THE SHAOLIN ATHLETE:

KUNG FU CONDITIONING FOR SPORTS, FITNESS, AND HEALTH

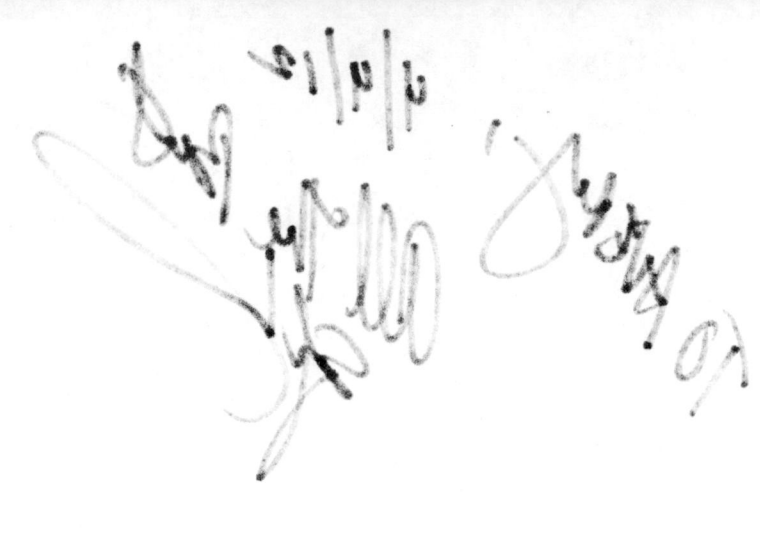

THE SHAOLIN ATHLETE:

KUNG FU CONDITIONING FOR SPORTS, FITNESS, AND HEALTH

By Sifu Karl Romain and Dr. G. Steve Kinnard

The Shaolin Athlete—*Kung Fu Conditioning for Sports, Fitness, and Health*
Copyright ©2012 by Sifu Karl Romain and Dr. G. Steve Kinnard.

ISBN: 978-0-9849087-0-7

About the authors: World Champion and International Kung Fu Hall of Fame inductee, **Sifu Karl Romain**, has been studying and training in Kung Fu for 34 years. He is also an instructor in T'ien Shan Pai Yang Style Tai Chi Chuan. Sifu Romain is the owner and master instructor of the Edgewater Kung Fu Academy in Edgewater, New Jersey. Sifu Romain has made several television appearances on the Dr. Oz Show, the Oprah Show, NBC 1st Look, ESPN, and Good Day New York. Sifu Romain is highly qualified to write *The Shaolin Athlete* because he worked as an off-season coach for the New York Giants football team and mentored former wide receiver Amani Toomer in his productive career with the Giants.

    Dr. Steve Kinnard is a student of Sifu Karl Romain. Dr. Kinnard earned a black sash in Shaolin Northern Long Fist Kung Fu. He has served as an assistant instructor in Sifu Romain's Academy. He also practices Tai Chi Chuan. Sifu Romain and Dr. Kinnard developed a Kung Fu leadership program for at-risk youth. The book that accompanies this program is entitled, *The Cross and the Warrior*. Dr. Kinnard is a teacher and evangelist with the New York City Church of Christ. He is an Adjunct Professor of Bible and Theology at Lincoln Christian University. He is the author of over ten books.

THEATRON PRESS publishes books which promote health, fitness, wellness, and responsible stewardship of the gift of life. For more information about Theatron Press, you may contact the publisher at toneyipibooks@mac.com.

Cover and interior design: Toney C. Mulhollan

THEATRON PRESS
An imprint of Illumination Publishers International
6010 Pinecreek Ridge Court
Spring, Texas 77379 • USA
www.Theatron-Press.com
www.ipibooks.com

TABLE OF CONTENTS

DISCLAIMER

Please note that the authors and publisher of this book are NOT RESPONSIBLE in any manner whatsoever for any injury that may result from practicing the techniques and/or following the instructions given within. Kung Fu Conditioning can be dangerous. Some of the physical activities described herein may be too strenuous or otherwise inappropriate for some readers. It is essential that the reader consult his or her personal physician before attempting to practice any of the techniques and/or follow any of the instructions in this book.

DEDICATION

Sifu Romain graciously dedicates this book to:
My instructors: Sifu Phil Sant and Grandmaster Willy Lin

Dr. Kinnard lovingly dedicates this book to:
Leigh, Chelsea, and Daniel.
Thanks for taking this journey with me.

ACKNOWLEDGEMENTS

"WHEN DRINKING WATER, DON'T FORGET WHO DUG THE WELL."
—TRADITIONAL CHINESE PROVERB

Special thanks from Sifu Romain and Dr. Kinnard to:

Toney Mulhollan for your work editing, formatting, and designing the book.

Sije Jodie Taylor for your help with photography and design.

Amani Toomer, Jiao Lian Dean Mendelson, Jiao Lian Cynthia Rosenberger, and Chelsea Kinnard for demonstrating the forms and exercises.

Une-Hi Song for your contribution to the book.

Special thanks from Sifu Romain to:

Lisa Oz for your support, encouragement, friendship, and suggestions on improving the book.

Dr. Oz for your friendship and allowing me to share my knowledge with your audience.

Amani Toomer for being a great student and friend. Congrats on having a great career.

Howard Cross for introducing me to Amani and for your friendship and support through the years.

Sifu Phil Sant of the ACCS for all the encouragement and the knowledge you have shared with me.

Greg Najac for your support and encouragement over the years.

Grandmaster Willy Lin for sharing your knowledge with me and for your support.

Sifu Linda Morrissey, Jen Brown, and my staff at Edgewater Kung Fu for sharing my vision of building excellent martial arts academies that will influence the lives of thousands of students.

Thanks to my parents, Claude and Louis; my brother, Pierre; and my sister, Fab. Thanks for always being there for me.

And a very special thanks to my daughter, Hope. You are my never-ending source of inspiration.

Thanks to Dr. G. Steve Kinnard for all your hard work and not giving up on this project.

Special thanks from Dr. G. Steve Kinnard to:

Sifu Karl Romain.
Sifu Linda Morrissey.
The elders, staff, and members of the New York City Church of Christ.
CLBK, CDK, DSK.

PART I

INTRODUCTION TO THE SHAOLIN ATHLETE

One who is good at being a warrior
does not make a show of his might;
One who is good in battle does not get angry.

—Lao Tzu

CHAPTER ONE

KUNG FU CONDITIONING:

THE PATHWAY TO SUCCESS IN ATHLETICS AND IN LIFE

The Way is in training…
Do nothing which is not of value.[1]
—Miyamoto Musashi

In any sport, there are good athletes, great athletes, and the best of the best. This book will help you be the best of the best in your sport. But *The Shaolin Athlete* is not just for the serious athlete. Everyone can learn about proper health and conditioning, both for sports and for life, in *The Shaolin Athlete*. This is because the Kung Fu Conditioning exercises taught in *The Shaolin Athlete* target the body, the mind, and the spirit as a whole. The Shaolin Athlete/Kung Fu Conditioning program is the complete fitness and health program for everyone, from the professional athlete to the weekend warrior to the average Jane or Joe who wants to get in better shape and live longer. Kung Fu Conditioning is for fitness, health, conditioning, and longevity.

Serious athletes are always looking for a competitive advantage. In today's world, everyone is looking for a way to excel and succeed. One of the most important factors in a professional athlete's success is his or her conditioning. We are not just speaking of physical conditioning. Mental conditioning is just as important as physical conditioning. This book was written with the serious athlete in mind, but it was also written for anyone who wants to succeed in life. Life and athletics closely parallel each other. The lessons we learn from athletics can help us in every aspect of life.

The Shaolin Athlete provides conditioning exercises and positive mental training exercises that can equip you to succeed in life. Kung Fu Conditioning is not a new, hip fitness fad. This book contains physical and mental conditioning exercises that have been practiced for the past 1,500 years. Shaolin Kung Fu warriors practiced these exercises to give them the edge they needed to survive in battle. They became some of the most elite warriors that the world has ever known. They passed their secrets down from generation to generation within their communities. Today you can use the secrets of Kung Fu Conditioning exercises to make you a better athlete and to get that added edge that will set you apart from your competition.

Would you like to be a better athlete? Would you like to succeed in business? Do you want to be a better parent? Are you thinking of improving your self-esteem? Would you like to be able to give back to your community or your neighborhood? Are you looking to live a longer, healthier life? Do you want to overcome insecurity? Do you want to stay young longer? If you answered any of these questions with a "yes," then *The Shaolin Athlete* is for you.

Get ready to embark on a journey that will reshape your life.

WHAT IS KUNG FU CONDITIONING?

"Understanding and cultivating the warrior spirit is what true martial training is all about." [2]
—Forrest E. Morgan, Retired Major USAF

"The real secret to becoming an expert in martial arts is realizing that training is a process of self-discovery." [3]
—Nicklaus Suino, author and martial artist

Kung Fu Conditioning turns athletes into better athletes by using Shaolin Kung Fu Conditioning exercises to strengthen specific skill areas and muscle groups, based on the individual athlete's need in his or her sport. Athletes come to their sport with certain attributes that enable them to play that sport at the top level. These attributes might include speed, power, or agility. Kung Fu Conditioning targets the attributes of the individual athlete and strengthens the key areas in off-the-field training sessions, translating to a better performance on the field.

What is good for professional athletes is good for anyone who wants to be in better condition or in better health. Kung Fu conditioning covers a wide range of areas, for example:

- strengthening muscle groups
- increasing flexibility
- improving breathing and breath control
- strengthening joints
- creating elasticity in joints
- developing concentration
- improving focus
- cultivating chi energy
- increasing clarity
- increasing a positive mental attitude

Kung Fu conditioning can address each area with specific, ancient Kung Fu, Tai Chi, and Chi Gong exercises that can strengthen the target area.

Here is a sampling of the features of Kung Fu Conditioning:

1. Kung Fu Conditioning trains your body the way that most sports are played—with quick starts and stops.

Most sports require the athlete to expend quick bursts of energy over a short period of time. Think of a shortstop diving to stop a line drive. Or think of a football receiver running a sideline pattern and extending his arms to make a catch right at the sideline. Or think of a tennis player ending the volley with a forehand smash that bounces just inside the line. Kung Fu Conditioning is designed to enable the athlete to develop the ability to expend short and quick, yet extremely powerful bursts of energy to achieve specific goals. And what applies to sports often applies to life. To make it in life, you have to be able to think fast and to react fast. Kung Fu Conditioning trains the student to react quickly and powerfully.

2. Kung Fu Conditioning will give you a holistic workout.

Kung Fu Conditioning conditions the whole athlete—his or her body, mind, emotions, and spirit. A central tenet of Kung Fu Conditioning is the harmony of body, mind, and spirit. This is a holistic approach to conditioning.

As you strengthen your body, you also strengthen your mind, your attitude, your emotions, and your spirit. For example, a stationary stance like the *Ma Bu* (the horse stance) works as a great physical strengthening exercise. Dropping into and holding a horse stance is like squatting 300 lbs. But the horse stance also teaches endurance. It teaches mental and emotional toughness. It teaches muscle memory. It teaches the "Yes, I Can" attitude. Kung Fu Conditioning is built on this holistic approach to exercise.

3. Kung Fu Conditioning doesn't get boring.

Many forms of exercise grow stale and boring over time. Wouldn't it be great if you could find an alternative to hitting the weight room? Kung Fu Conditioning provides that alternative. It can strengthen your muscles without weights. And since it is more than fifteen hundred years old, there is an endless universe of material to learn and explore as you improve your conditioning and become a better athlete and a better person.

4. Kung Fu Conditioning will strengthen the athletic attributes that are most important for your particular sport.

What attribute is most essential for you to be great at your sport? Is it speed? Is it hand/eye coordination? Is it flexibility? Is it power, or is it endurance? Kung Fu Conditioning targets the exact attribute that you need to work on to be better at your sport.

5. Kung Fu Conditioning is great for athletes who are looking for a cross-training regime.

Recent studies in sports fitness and conditioning have shown the importance of cross-training. Marathon runners are now riding bikes to increase their peak performance. Golfers are lifting weights. Kung Fu Conditioning is the ultimate tool for cross-training. You won't need to go to the weight room. You won't need the stationary bike. Kung Fu Conditioning can provide a cardiovascular workout. It can give you an aerobic and an anaerobic workout.

6. Kung Fu Conditioning will give you greater endurance by teaching you how to breathe properly.

7. Kung Fu Conditioning is a positive, affirming workout.

The Shaolin Athlete becomes a better person, as he or she becomes a better athlete.

8. Kung Fu Conditioning builds functional muscles.

The great Kung Fu artist Bruce Lee used to talk about functional muscles. A functional muscle is defined as a muscle that works properly regardless of the sport you play. Kung Fu Conditioning develops functional muscles.

9. Kung Fu Conditioning is not a fad.

The martial arts have been around for thousands of years. This is not a "here today, gone tomorrow" conditioning program. The Shaolin monks took their conditioning very seriously because they weren't just conditioning themselves to play a sport to win a trophy. They were battling to keep their culture alive and to protect their community, their families, their friends, and their temple. Kung Fu Conditioning has been here for at least 1,500 years. It will be here 1,500 more. Fitness trends come and go, but Kung Fu Conditioning is here to stay.

Can Kung Fu Conditioning Help Me Regardless of the Sport I Play?

The short answer is, "Yes!" If you are an athlete, then Kung Fu Conditioning can help you improve in your sport. Even if you aren't an athlete, Kung Fu Conditioning can help you. Kung Fu Conditioning is beneficial for everyone.

Someone protests, "But I'm a golfer. How can Kung Fu Conditioning help me?" Answer: The waist turn is one of the most important aspects of golf. Tai Chi and Bagua have exercises that specifically target not just the waist, but the turning of the waist.

Someone else protests, "But I'm a marathon runner. How can Kung Fu Conditioning help me be a better distance runner?" Answer: Kung Fu teaches breathing techniques that will greatly benefit your running. Plus, have you ever hit the wall while running? Kung Fu Conditioning will prepare you mentally so that you can break through the wall.

Kung Fu training exercises target specific body parts and specific muscle groups. No matter what sport you play, there are Kung Fu Conditioning exercises that can help you perform better at your sport. For example, a wide receiver in football needs to develop hand speed and hand strength. There are specific Kung Fu exercises that target these areas.

A baseball catcher needs a strong core and strong leg muscles. Kung Fu Conditioning has training exercises that target the core and the leg muscles. An ice skater needs long, lean, flexible muscles that can bend and stretch. There are Kung Fu Conditioning exercises that work on making muscles and joints more flexible. No matter what sport you play, Kung Fu Conditioning has something that can help you reach your maximum potential in that sport.

For an athlete to be successful, he or she must exhibit superior abilities in several athletic skills. An athlete must be as strong as an ox, as quick as a cheetah, and as agile as a monkey. Kung Fu training exercises can target specific skill areas and help strengthen these areas. The Kung Fu exercises found in this book target the following areas:

- **flexibility**
- **power**
- **balance and control**
- **coordination**

- **speed**
- **agility/mobility**
- **strength/power**
- **endurance/stamina**
- **focus**
- **confidence**
- **sensitivity and awareness**
- **reaction time**

Kung Fu training can also target specific muscle groups. Different muscles groups are more or less important depending on the sport that a person plays, or even on the position that someone plays in a sport. For example, a point guard in the NBA isn't going to have the same muscle mass as an NFL lineman. A tennis player isn't going to have the same body type as a rugby player. Each athlete needs to be able to focus on specific muscle groups that are important to his or her own success within their sport.

Kung Fu Conditioning targets specific muscle groups. For example:

- **lower body—legs, knees, and feet**
- **core—the abdomen**
- **hip**
- **back**
- **upper body—shoulders and chest**
- **upper body—arms**
- **neck**

No matter what sport you play, whether baseball or soccer, football or swimming, wrestling or tennis, skiing or gymnastics, ice hockey or basketball, boxing or cycling, Kung Fu Conditioning can help you be more competitive at your sport. These methods have been tested and have proven to be successful. Kung Fu Conditioning can help you reach your full potential in your sport.

What If I'm Not a Serious Athlete, But Just Someone Who Is Trying To Be Fit?

Even if you aren't a serious athlete, Kung Fu Conditioning is for you. It can literally change your life. It can change your life because it is a holistic approach to conditioning which conditions the body, mind, and spirit. Kung Fu Conditioning makes a person tougher physically, mentally, emotionally, and spiritually. You start where you are. You work on your weaknesses and change those weaknesses into strengths. Kung Fu Conditioning is for young and old, professional athlete or weekend warrior, woman or man, boy or girl, the tough guy or the not-so-tough guy. Kung Fu Conditioning is for anyone who wants to get in better shape and to enjoy life more.

How Much Time Will I Need To Devote to Kung Fu Conditioning?

That depends on what you want to do with your conditioning. A serious athlete needs to have a body that is in top physical shape. The casual athlete doesn't need to devote as much time. But since Kung Fu Conditioning targets specific areas that you as an individual need to improve, the time spent in Kung Fu Conditioning is qualitatively time well spent when compared to just hitting the weights in the weight room or running some laps on the track.

Kung Fu Conditioning is an excellent supplement to your regularly scheduled practice days for your sport. It is a great cross-training tool. If you're waiting for your season to open, Kung Fu Conditioning can help you enter training camp in better condition than you've ever attained before.

Kung Fu Conditioning sessions can accomplish more in thirty minutes than you could accomplish in two hours in the weight room or on the track. The Shaolin Athlete program begins with specific calisthenics to get the heart rate up, followed by focused work on precise areas targeted to make you a better athlete. All of this can be accomplished in thirty to forty-five minute sessions, two or three times a week.

But again, you have look at your individual goals. What do you want to accomplish? Setting your own personal goals and reaching those goals is the most important consideration in determining how much time you spend and how many days you practice Kung Fu Conditioning.

CHAPTER TWO

AMANI TOOMER, THE NEW YORK GIANTS, AND THE CHAMPIONSHIP SEASON

Moving, be like water. Still, be like a mirror.
Respond like an echo.[4]

—Bruce Lee

Kung Fu Conditioning has been field-tested. Amani Toomer, former wide receiver of the New York Giants, tested it. Then, at the beginning of the 1999–2000 NFL football season, Coach Jim Fassel invited me (Sifu Karl Romain) to add Kung Fu Conditioning exercises to the training program of the New York Giants football team.

SIFU ROMAIN AND THE CHAMPIONSHIP SEASON

In the year 2000, the New York Football Giants went to the Super Bowl. Under the direction of Coach Jim Fassel, the Giants won the National Football Conference Championship and headed to the biggest event in the sporting world. You might have heard of the on-the-field contributions of some of the members of that team—Michael Strahan, Amani Toomer, Tiki Barber, Keith Hamilton, and Howard Cross. But you probably haven't heard how Kung Fu Conditioning played a part in that championship season. This Kung Fu Conditioning story is the off-the-field story. It happened in the training room, before the players ever set foot on the playing field.

New York Giants linebacker, Howard Cross, was the first Giant to train in our Kung Fu Conditioning program. Mr. Cross began his training at Karl Romain's Kung Fu Academy in Nyack, New York. In the Giants locker room, Mr. Cross was talking about what he was learning in his training sessions. Giants wide receiver Amani Toomer overheard Mr. Cross talking about his Kung Fu training. Amani mentioned to Mr. Cross that his dad had trained in the martial arts, and that he was very interested in taking some lessons. So Amani joined us in some Kung Fu Conditioning classes.

Mr. Toomer later said that taking the Kung Fu Conditioning class was the toughest thing he had ever done in his life. At first he didn't want to come back, but then he saw that the challenge he faced physically and mentally in the Kung Fu Conditioning class was not available anywhere else, and he decided to come back. He saw how Kung Fu Conditioning would make him a better athlete. After he had studied the martial arts for a while, he grew to appreciate how studying the martial arts helped him in his career, and how it gave him a different perception of what he was doing on the football field.

At the end of the 1999 season, several Giants players were interested in taking Kung Fu Conditioning classes. Mr. Cross and Mr. Toomer had shared about their Kung Fu Conditioning experience with several members of the team. Some of the players began to see how Kung Fu Conditioning would benefit their football careers.

Before I (Sifu Romain) knew it, I had a meeting scheduled with the head coach of the New York Giants, Jim Fassel. I can remember walking into the Giants office and thinking, "Wow, I'm actually here!" I sat down with Coach Fassel and he asked me straight out, "What is the benefit of Kung Fu?" He also asked me, "What can you do to benefit the team? How can you help with hand speed and coordination?" These were all great questions.

I explained to Coach Fassel, "I'm not a football player, and I can't teach your players how to play football better, but I can help them with their physical attributes. I can show them how to focus and how to improve their speed. I can help them with their coordination and get them to jump a little higher and move a little faster. By working on their athletic attributes, I can help them perform better at football.

The basic difference between a good-to-great and a great-to-elite athlete is the toning of their physical attributes and their attitude. I can help improve attributes like speed, focus, agility, and coordination so that the good athlete can become an elite athlete. I can also teach them the warrior attitude."

So I began working with the Giants in their preseason training sessions, and they went on to win the NFC championship. They finished that season playing in the Super Bowl.

> I learned many valuable lessons from that Super Bowl season with the Giants. One lesson I learned is that all athletes are the same regardless of the sport. We are all trying to be the best we can be. We all have periods of high confidence and periods of low confidence. We are all looking for that little edge that will set us apart from the competition. That little edge, whether it be mental, physical, emotional, or spiritual is incredibly important.
>
> Another lesson I learned is that when it comes to organized team sports, it is all about creating team spirit and developing synergy. The more you can get people to work together and see things from a common perspective, the more you will accomplish as a team.

As I worked with the Giants, I focused on a few specific areas where I knew that Kung Fu Conditioning would greatly enhance their abilities as athletes. I worked on improving their balance, speed, and coordination. I gave them some martial arts techniques that they could take and translate into their play on the football field. For example, Michael Strahan was very fond of *Hubud*, an energy drill taken from the Filipino martial arts. Hubud develops responsiveness in the athlete. Mr. Strahan used this technique to help him break through the offensive line to get to the quarterback. Mr. Toomer used the same technique to free himself from defensive backs so that he could run his pass patterns.

Since that 2000 championship season, I have continued to work with Howard Cross, Amani Toomer, and offensive tackle Ian Allen. Mr. Allen told me that he has enjoyed Kung Fu Conditioning because it has helped him with his focus/concentration, endurance and hand speed. It also has helped him with his mindset. It has taught him how to perceive things in a new and different way.

My experience with the Giants in the 2000 championship season is a prime example of how Kung Fu Conditioning can help professional athletes get more from their training and conditioning programs. We work with athletes to improve their physical attributes. When these attributes improve, the result is seen on the playing field.

Amani Toomer and Kung Fu Conditioning

The August 2, 2003, a news clip on TeamGiants.com reported:

> Amani Toomer has spent much of his past six years training at Romain's Kung Fu. He takes lessons twice a week all year long, even during football season. He earned his black belt this summer. Toomer says Kung Fu deserves much of the credit for his performance last season, when he caught a career-high 82 passes for 1,334 yards. He also used the martial arts to stay in shape this summer, making him an early standout at training camp. "Pretty much everything he does on the field can be related back to what we work on together," said Karl Romain, Toomer's instructor. "He's learned better reaction time, better flexibility, better patience, and better attitude here." It's no coincidence, then, that Toomer's career blossomed shortly after he walked into Romain's Kung Fu. Toomer learned about the place from former teammate Howard Cross and decided to check it out for himself in 1997. In 1998, Toomer's season numbers improved slightly— by 11 catches and about 100 receiving yards. After that season, Toomer increased his Kung Fu lessons to four times a week. In 1999, his numbers ballooned as he accumulated more than 1,000 yards receiving for the first time in his career."[5]

In this report, Mr. Toomer gives credit to Kung Fu Conditioning for his success as an athlete.

ESPN did an interview with Amani Toomer and Sifu Karl Romain at Edgewater Kung Fu in Edgewater, New Jersey. They entitled this piece, "Crouching Giant, Hidden Ninja."[6] The interviewer asked Mr. Toomer, "How does Kung Fu translate to football?" Mr. Toomer responded, "With breathing exercises, a lot of stuff that you do, little tricks that you learn, …these translate into what I can do on the field. When I'm getting pressed by a defensive back, they try to come at me, …I use my moves to try and get away from them. Once you get used to hands coming at you, it is easier once it comes in a game." Mr. Toomer clearly states how Kung Fu Conditioning Exercises translates to success on the playing field.

The interviewer asked Mr. Toomer, "After your first class of Kung Fu, what did you think?" Mr. Toomer responded with a smile, "Oh, no, I am not coming back. Because it was so hard. I was standing in one spot, and holding my arms out for a little while. And my arms started to shake and you ask yourself, 'What's going on? I lift weights; I'm in pretty good shape.' And it totally changed my perspective on things."

The interviewer said to Mr. Toomer, "Coach Fassel saw such a marked improvement in you that he asked Karl (Sifu Romain) to actually come out and teach the team, how did that go?" Mr. Toomer responded, "I think it went pretty well. I think some of the skill players and the position players were participating in it. And that year we ended up going to the Super Bowl. I don't know if that had a direct correlation, but I'd like to think so."

The benefit of Kung Fu Conditioning for Mr. Toomer's career as a professional football player can best be illustrated by citing material in two articles from the Sports section of the *New York Times*. The first article was written in August 1998, which was toward the beginning of Mr. Toomer's career just after Sifu Romain began working with him. The second article, written in October 2007, highlighted many of the accomplishments of Mr. Toomer during his seasons with the New York Giants. Both articles detail the benefit of Kung Fu Conditioning for Mr. Toomer's career. Written almost ten years apart, by two different authors, published by one of our nation's greatest newspapers, these two articles serve as a testimony to the enduring contribution that Mr. Toomer has made to the New York Giants. The articles also document the impact that Kung Fu Conditioning has had on Mr. Toomer's athletic career.

From "A Whole New Look for Giants' Toomer," by Bill Pennington, *The New York Times*, August 9, 1998.

> When the Giants' season ended last year, the team's coaches gathered to evaluate the roster. In those meetings, it was agreed that Amani Toomer, the wide receiver the Giants had drafted with great promise just two years ago, might not be in the team's plans much longer.
> The Giants were going to draft two wide receivers. There was a good

chance Toomer would be cut in training camp….

The Giants opened their preseason last night, defeating the visiting Cincinnati Bengals, and the same coaches who felt they could probably do without Toomer are now calling him the team's most improved player.

Day after day this summer, a coach or a teammate has referred to Toomer as "a changed man."

Whether he is using a new, more physical playing style to battle hefty linebackers for passes, or outracing cornerbacks down the sideline for long touchdown passes, or running precise, clever pass routes across the middle, Toomer has been the unquestioned star of camp….

"There is something seriously wrong with you if you haven't noticed the difference in Amani," Giants safety Sam Garnes said. "He's a terror out there."

Quarterback Danny Kanell was watching the group of defensive backs and wide receivers run end-of-practice sprints the other day. These are the fleetest of Giants, the team thoroughbreds.

"I remember last year when Amani was struggling just to finish the sprints," Kanell said. "I looked up the other day and he was racing Jason Sehorn at the front of the pack, shoulder to shoulder. Jason is the best-conditioned guy on the team."

"It's like a totally different man has shown up in Amani's uniform."

Actually, the 6-foot-2-inch, 200-pound Toomer showed up in a different uniform. He ditched the No. 89 jersey he wore in his first two seasons with the Giants and has taken jersey No. 81…

No one is crediting the number change for the change in Toomer. The change has been a simple one, if you ask him, although he seems embarrassed when asked what it's like to be a changed man.

"Of course, I'm the same person," said Toomer, who is quiet and reserved. "I just wasn't putting my best foot forward most of the time. I knew I had to do a lot more and I had to be more focused about what I wanted to achieve."

He also knew Fassel thought he was failing as a football player.
"I had to prove to him and everybody else that I did know what I was doing," the 23-year-old Toomer said. "That's what drove me."

The first thing Toomer did in his make over was attend the team's off-season strength and conditioning program every day it was scheduled and some days when it wasn't.

"He worked harder than anybody," Fassel said. "He worked so hard I found myself pulling for him—really pulling for him."

Toomer also took kung fu instruction in nearby Nyack, N.Y. "Their training exercises really strengthened my knee," Toomer said, referring to his right knee, which was surgically repaired in 1996 after he tore his anterior cruciate ligament. "In kung fu there are some very low stances and you need strength and flexibility at the same time to be able to do the movements."

"It's allowed me to play lower on the football field. I think I'm coming off the cuts faster."[7]

In this preceding article you see where Mr. Toomer specifically credits his Kung Fu training at Karl Romain's Kung Fu in Nyack with strengthening his knee. This is what Kung Fu Conditioning can do. It can target specific parts of the body that need to be strengthened in each individual athlete. Kung Fu Conditioning helped Amani Toomer get on the right track in his career with the Giants.

As you'll see in the next article (written almost ten years after the first one), Kung Fu Conditioning helped Mr. Toomer stay on track throughout his professional football career.

From "Giants' Toomer Excels With a Body of Work," by David Picker, *The New York Times*, October 18, 2007.

Amani Toomer's most impressive moment during the Giants' victory Monday night over the Atlanta Falcons was one of the following:

a) His seventh catch, which allowed him to pass Tiki Barber for most career receptions as a Giant (587).

b) His 5-yard touchdown catch, which tied him with Kyle Rote for most touchdown receptions as a Giant (48).

c) His 17-yard reception to the Falcons' 1-yard line on which he grazed his toes inbounds with a centimeter to spare.

d) None of the above.

The answer might be d.

In the second quarter Toomer burst off the line of scrimmage and immediately ran into cornerback DeAngelo Hall. Some receivers would have gotten flustered by the tight coverage. Not Toomer, a black belt in kung fu. He repeatedly chopped his arms like an oil rig and brushed past Hall and caught a 15-yard pass. The Giants scored on the next play en route to a 31-10 victory.

"If somebody's grabbing me, trying to jam me, I can get off pretty quick," Toomer said Wednesday when asked if his martial-arts skills translated to football. "I can block out everything else and just have one train of thought."

Toomer, a 12-year veteran, began learning kung fu a year after being drafted by the Giants in 1996. Inspired by his father, who won several trophies in karate when Toomer was a child, he earned his black belt about four years ago. [8]

Kung Fu Conditioning helped Mr. Toomer in the beginning of his career to become a better athlete, and it helped him to have longevity as an athlete.

Amani Toomer is the all-time leading pass receiver for the NY Football Giants (9,497 yards). He is a Super Bowl champion. He also is a Shaolin Athlete. He gives his own testimonial about Kung Fu Conditioning in these words:

In 1997, I walked into Sifu Karl Romain's Kung Fu Academy as a 22 year old, very confident football player who thought he was at the top of his game. But one hour into the workout I realized two things: first, I'm never coming back to this Kung Fu class again; and second, I had a lot to learn.

That epiphany opened my mind to new things. It not only opened my mind to Kung Fu, but it also made me rethink all aspects of my life. Football became a much more enjoyable passion for me. Kung Fu forced me to evaluate myself as a player, and it also forced me to be honest with myself concerning my abilities and my shortcomings.

With the help of Sifu Karl Romain I was able not only to work on my shortcomings and become a more accountable football player, but also to fall in love with the process and not just fall in love with the success. I learned to love every step that it took for me to succeed in the NFL.

Sifu Romain was more than just a Kung Fu instructor to me, he was a mentor. He mentored me and taught me what it was like to overcome his neck injury, and I myself ended up having to overcome a knee injury. Dealing with the particular hardships that athletes deal with when it comes to those types of injuries, career-ending types of injuries, it really shed a positive light on my career. He taught me great lessons in terms of resiliency and stick-to-itiveness, which directly correlated into my career with the Giants. [9]

—From a message to the authors on January 29, 2012

Mr. Toomer recognizes the contribution that Kung Fu Conditioning made to his long and illustrious career with the NY Football Giants. Jeremy Booth of *Inside Kung Fu Magazine* writes, "It's no accident that Amani Toomer's rise to NFL prominence coincided with his kung-fu training. Determination, steel nerves, explosive power, fast feet and accurate hands—whether in self-defense or in competition, martial artists are forever searching for this state of physical and mental synchrony. The martial arts community has long understood that diligent practice builds these skills, which then can be applied to a vast array of life's situations."[10] Kung Fu helped Amani Toomer reach his goals as a professional athlete. Kung Fu Conditioning can help you reach your goals in sports and in life.

NEW YORK FOOTBALL GIANTS

Dear Karl,   6/29/00

The New York Giants and myself would like to thank you for all your help
this spring. One of our goals this off-season was to improve team quickness,
balance and focus. From the response of our players we feel as though we
were successful. Personally, I would like to thank you as well. The
information you provided our players was outstanding. Not only did our
players improve, I also benefited. Over the past 17 years in the NFL I've
had the opportunity to work with and learn from several Martial artists and
you were by far the best I've had the pleasure to work with. Your ability to
instruct and motivate our players was exceptional. I wish you the best of
luck and look forward to working with you again in the future.

John "Mother" Dunn

Strength & Conditioning Coach
New York Giants

GIANTS STADIUM • EAST RUTHERFORD, NJ 07073 • EXECUTIVE OFFICES: 201-935-8111 • TICKET OFFICE: 201-935-8222 • FAX: 201-939-4134

WORLD CHAMPIONS 1927 1934 1938 1956 1986 1990   NFC CHAMPIONS 1986 1990   NFC EAST CHAMPIONS 1986 1989 1990 1997
EASTERN CHAMPIONS 1933 1934 1935 1938 1939 1941 1944 1946 1956 1958 1959 1961 1962 1963

PART II

KUNG FU CONDITIONING: THE PROGRAM

Do Not move unless it is advantageous.
Do not execute unless it is effective.
Do not challenge unless it is critical.[11]

—SUN TZU

CONDITIONING AND TRAINING EXERCISES

This section of the book focuses on some of the specific Kung Fu Conditioning exercises that will help you become a Shaolin athlete and will help you realize all the goals you have set as an athlete. Before we introduce the specific conditioning exercises, we first want to mention and define the physical attributes and muscle groups that the Kung Fu Conditioning exercises will target.

Attributes that Kung Fu Conditioning targets:

Flexibility

The ability to bend without breaking. Also, flexibility is the ability to be fluid and mobile in movement. *The Eight Skills of Kung Fu* states, "Twist your waist as a snake." Sang H. Kim in his book *Ultimate Flexibility* writes, "Flexibility is the ability to move your muscles and joints through their full range of motion. When it comes to martial arts, the range of motion required for advanced movements often calls for greater than average flexibility. One of the first things you learn as a martial artist is how to stretch your muscles to increase your flexibility." [12] Sifu Romain states, "In our Kung Fu Conditioning classes, I stress to the students that you need flexibility not only physically, but also in your mind. I tell my students that Bruce Lee use to say, 'No way is way.' You have to be flexible in your approach to life, and in remaining flexible, you become teachable."

Power

The Eight Skills of Kung Fu states, "Set your feet on the ground as if fastened by strong glue." When strength is used with a quick, sudden burst of energy, this is power. A football lineman uses power when he fires off the line to block a defensive player. Power is seen in jumps, kicks, sprints, and knockout punches. In Kung Fu, true power comes from the root. It comes from the stance. Can you stand your ground against attacks? Constant training of this physical root power leads to power throughout your life, which can be called personal power. This is power within you that gives you the ability to overcome obstacles and challenges in life. It teaches you how to endure in life. It teaches you to persist until you succeed.

Balance and Control

You achieve balance when you use muscular control to remain steady. Balance is critical for an athlete. It is seen when a gymnast works on a balance beam or when a wide receiver steps just inside the lines to stay in bounds after a catch. Watch some of the catches that former Giants wide receiver Amani Toomer made over the years and you'll see balance demonstrated. He knew where he was on the field. He knew how to control the ball and how to control his body. This is balance.

Athletes need to learn balance both on and off the field. It is easy to become obsessed with new fads and gimmicks. You can quickly go from one extreme to another. You can start by not working out at all and then become consumed by working out to the point of injuring yourself. Balance helps us control our schedules. It helps us find the time in our schedules not only to work out, but also to rest and to get proper nourishment. Balance helps us make sure that we are not just growing physically, but that we are also growing mentally, emotionally, and spiritually.

Speed

Fast movement. *The Eight Skills of Kung Fu* states, "Swing your fists as fast as the meteor flies." In sports, "speed kills." Bruce Lee in his book *Jeet Kune Do* writes, "Speed and more speed, greater and greater mobility." [13] In order to have speed, the body must be relaxed. In order to relax, you have to learn how to breathe properly. If an athlete is slow, it does not make for superior results. Speed can be learned. The key to being fast is to learn how to relax more. Even though you are moving with intensity, you stay relaxed.

Agility/Mobility

Agility is a combination of skills—speed, balance, quickness and suppleness—that allows the athlete to move with great skill. Think of a point guard in basketball who weaves between defenders to get the ball in position to make an assist.

Strength/Power

The ability to withstand or to exert force and pressure. Strength is focused power. Wrestlers use strength to struggle against their opponent as they look for an opportunity to take their opponent to the mat. In football, strength and power allow an offensive lineman to open a hole in the defensive line for the running back to gain yardage.

Endurance/Stamina

The ability to bear prolonged exertion or pain. This is the ability to persist. It is the mindset which says, "I will, until." Think of a marathon runner who pounds the pavement for 26.2 miles. Think of the cyclist who pushes pedal over pedal for 150 miles. Think of the martial artist who after three hours of training, sinks into and holds the horse stance for five minutes.

An elite athlete has to endure not just the physical trauma of sports, but he or she also has to endure the mental and emotional side of sports. You are dealing with fans, coaches, contracts, the media, agents, money, and relationships. You have to do all of this while realizing that no one really cares about anything except your last performance as an athlete. Being an athlete requires that you persevere. Being an athlete requires the ability to take great punishment without quitting. Success is not always about winning. Success is about learning how to push through the losses until you become a winner. You don't really fail until you stop trying. You have to have the stamina to rise from your failures and say, "I will persist until I succeed."

Focus

The ability to concentrate on a single task. You concentrate all of your attention on a single detail without being distracted. Think of a basketball player who is asked to hit a game-winning free throw on the opponent's court. Thousands of fans are shouting against this one player. He or she has to block out all the negativity and focus on hitting the shot.

Coordination

The integration of all the muscles and all the parts of the body to create fluidity of movement. In his *Tao of Jeet Kune Do*, Bruce Lee writes, "Coordination is by all means one of the most important considerations in any study of proficiency in sports and athletics. Coordination is the quality which enables the individual to integrate all the powers and capacities of his whole organism into an effective doing of an act."[14] *The Eight Skills of Kung Fu* teaches, "Use your strength naturally." This naturalness is coordination. The best athlete can coordinate all her attributes together so that she can run, jump, skip, leap, hop, or slide to make a play. Coordination pulls all the other attributes together, which leads to a superior athlete.

Sensitivity/Awareness

An athlete needs to be aware of his or her surroundings at all times. There are moments when the athlete needs to sense where the opponents are. The athlete must also be able to respond quickly to stimulation. Sensitivity training can heighten the athlete's reflexes. Awareness is as much mental as it is physical. The athlete must be trained to listen.

Confidence

Believing in yourself. If you don't believe in yourself, then who will believe in you? A winning athlete is a confident athlete, prepared in body, mind, and spirit to enter the game with skills honed to their peak so that she or he can perform and win.

Reaction Time

Elite athletes react quickly to their opponent. They read the opponent's move and respond with great agility. They can move in any direction. They act and react to their advantage on the field of play.

The Muscle Groups that Kung Fu Conditioning Targets

A. The Lower Body—Legs, Knees, and Feet: tensor fasciae lates, iliacus, psoas major, sartorius, gracilis, adductor longus, adductor magnus, biceps femoris semitendinousus, semimembranosus, extensor digitorum longus, soleus, peroneus tertius, tibialis anterior, gastrocnemius, flexor digitorum longus.

B. The Core—Abdomen: external oblique, rectus abdominis, internal oblique transverus.

C. The Hip: gluteus medius, gluteus minimus, gluteus maximus, tensor fasciae latae.

D. The Back: deltoid, trapezius, latissimus dorsi. These muscles are especially important in sports like swimming and rowing.

E. The Upper Body—Shoulder and Chest: pectoralis major, trapezius, subscapularis, supraspinatus, deltoid, infranspinatus.

F. The Upper Body—Arms: deltoid, biceps brachii, brachialis, triceps.

G. The Neck: semispinalis capitis, sternocleidomastoid, splenius capitis, longissimus capitis.

KUNG FU CONDITIONING EXERCISES AND TRAINING DRILLS

FEATURING AMANI TOOMER AND SIFU KARL ROMAIN

(THIS IS A SAMPLE WORKOUT OF SIFU ROMAIN WITH AMANI TOOMER. SOME OF THESE EXERCISES HAVE A MORE DETAILED EXPLANATION LATER IN THE BOOK. YOU WILL ALSO FIND TWO SAMPLE WORKOUTS THAT YOU CAN DO AT HOME.)

WARM UPS: HIGH KNEES

High Knees is good for stretching out the leg muscles and for circulating blood throughout the body at the beginning of a workout. High Knees is similar to running in place. The difference being that with high knees you intentionally focus on bringing the knees up to or beyond the waist before setting the foot back down on the floor. Place the palms in front of the body and focus on hitting the palms with the knees. The knees should go up and down rapidly. The higher you lift the knees and the quicker your pace, the greater the intensity to your workout.

WARM UPS: SWING LEG BACK

This exercise stretches out the leg muscles and loosens up the hamstring and back muscles. It also serves to condition the leg muscles. It also helps with balance and flexiblity. Begin by squatting down on the left leg and extending your right leg out in front of your body until it is parallel to the floor. Now push up to stand on your left leg and extend your right leg behind you. Reach your hands down behind your left calf muscle and pull your upper body toward the floor stretching your hamstring and lower back as you pull. Drop your head toward your left knee and extend your right leg up in the air to help with your balance. Slowly rise from the tucked position until your feet are back together and your hands are by your sides. Continue the exercise on the other side of the body.

WARM UPS: FRONT STRETCH KICKS

The Front Stretch Kick stretches the leg muscles and increases flexibility. Begin with feet together and arms stretched out in an iron cross stance. Focus the eyes on a spot in front of you that is about a foot above eye level. Your focus leads your intent. Place the right foot back. Your right toes should lightly touch the floor. Swing the right leg forward and up. Breathe out as you kick up. Once the leg is fully extended (as high as you can comfortably go), snap your leg back into place twice as fast. Do 10 front stretch kicks with the right leg. Then do 10 front stretch kicks with the left leg. You can perform front stretch kicks in one spot on the floor or by moving across the floor.

SPEED AND TIMING DRILLS:

These drills are excellent for strengthening reflexes and quickening reaction time. These are two person drills. Sifu Romain and Mr. Toomer sink into a horse stance. This quiets the lower body and isolates the work to the upper torso. Sifu Romain places his hands out with palms facing inward. Mr. Toomer makes a willow leaf palm with his hands. Mr. Toomer fires out a palm toward Sifu Romain's chest. Sifu Romain's objective is to catch Mr. Toomer's palm. The first three pictures illustrate this drill.

In the fourth picture, Mr. Toomer throws a single puch toward Sifu Romain. Sifu Romain softens his focus so that he sees the punch and follows the punch without blinking. This excercise works on focus. It also works on Mr. Toomer's speed, timing, and control as he fires the punch at Sifu Romain without hitting him.

FOCUS MITTS:

This is a two person drill that works on speed and reflexes. Sifu Romain is pictured holding the focus mitt. Mr. Toomer is pictured throwing a right jab at the mitt. Sifu Romain leads the drill. When he gives the word (a simple "Go" will suffice), Mr. Toomer throws the jab. Sifu Romain varies the count for when the punch is thrown. He also varies the location of the mitt. You can also mix it up by calling out for a jab or a cross or a jab-cross combination. This keeps Mr. Toomer on his toes, causing him to stay agile and focused. Thus the name—focus mitts.

Notice how Mr. Toomer turns his waist and pushes off his left toe to throw the cross.

HUBUD

Hubud is a two-person drill that works on the sensitivity, reflexes, speed, and focus. It works on a three movement pattern—deflect, push, and strike. When an opponent strikes, the defender deflects the attacks, pushes the attack away (or redirects the attack), and strikes back.

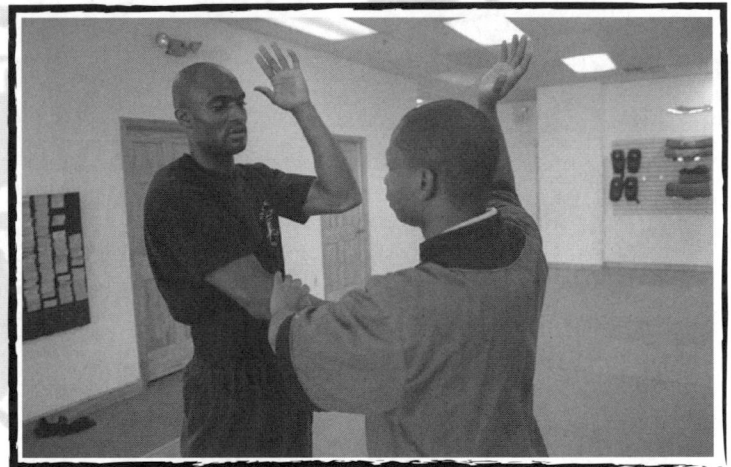

HUBUD

Sifu Romain deflects the attack.

Sift Romain redirects the attack, and throws a strike back toward Mr. Toomer.

Mr. Toomer deflects the attack, pushes it away, and strikes back. This quick attack and counter-attack exchange is great for building sensitivity and reflexes.

SHUAI CHIAO CHI GONG:

Shuai Chiao is Chinese Wresting. Chi Gong literally means energy work or energy exercise. Shuai Chiao Chi Gong is a set of exercises that strengthen the body specifically for the art of Chinese Wrestling. Chi Gong breathing is from the dantian. Breathe in and out through the nose with the tip of the tongue lightly touching the roof of the mouth.

THREE PLANES

The first exercise, Three Planes, strengthens the thighs, calves, forearms and fingers. Place your feet together. Bend on the knees and hips. The lower your bend, the harder the muscles will work to support you. This will greatly strengthen your lower body. Focus your eyes straight ahead. Bend your elbows and your wrists. Have each of your fingertips lightly touch the end of your thumb. This is known as a crane's beak. Quickly move your fingertips so they touch and release the thumb. Touch and release; touch and release. The faster you move your fingers, the harder the muscles in your forearms will work. When the fingers come together, inhale. When the fingers extend, exhale.

SHUAI CHIAO CHI GONG:

SHARPENING THE AX

Sharpening the Ax works the thighs, calves, forearms, upper arms, and fingers. Place your feet slightly over shoulder's width with the toes pointing forward. Drop into a low horse stance. Extend the arms directly in front of the chest and pull back on the wrists. The palms face outward and the fingertips are held together.

SHUAI CHIAO CHI GONG:

ANGEL STARING IN THE MIRROR

Angel Staring in the Mirror works on the thighs, calves, forearms, and fingers. Place feet in the right forward stance position. The back (left) leg is locked out and the forward (right) leg is bent at the knee. Try to get your right thigh parallel to the floor. The lower you drop the more you will work the leg muscles. Both hands form a crane's beak, meaning that your fingertips lightly touch the end of the thumb. Extend the right arm behind you. Bend your left arm at the elbow until your hand is in front of your face. Focus on the fingers of your left hand (this is the mirror). Quickly move your fingertips so they touch and release the thumb. Touch and release; touch and release. The faster you move your fingers, the harder the muscles in your forearms will work.

SHUAI CHIAO CHI GONG:
POINTING TO THE WINNER

Pointing to the Winner works on the thighs, the calves, the shoulders, the upper arms, and the forearms. Sifu Romain adjusts Mr. Toomer's arms to help him envision that he is holding a staff. Mr. Toomer is in a crane's stance. Raise the right foot off the floor and bend the knee. The left knee on the supporting leg should also be bent. The deeper you drop into this stance, the more you will work the leg muscles. Hold the right hand above the head and left hand at the waist. Imagine that you are holding a long staff in your hands. Focus straight ahead.

Once you have done this on one side, switch legs and work the other side.

SHUAI CHIAO CHI GONG:

RHINO WATCHING THE MOON

Rhino Watching the Moon works balance. It also stretches the back muscles, the calves, and the hamstrings. Cross the feet—left foot over the right. Make the right hand into a fist. Bring the right hand to chamber or to your pocket. Bend at the waist. Stretch your left arm around to your right calf. Try to reach behind your right calf. Stretch. Focus your eyes on your elevated elbow. You will have to fight to keep your balance. The more you bend and stretch; the more challenging this exercise becomes.

Once you have done this on one side, switch legs and work the other side.

SHUAI CHIAO CHI GONG:
COMBINED LYING STANCE

The Combined Lying Stance works the thighs, the calves, the shoulders, and the arms. Extend the feet out past the shoulders. Bend at the knees, bend at the hips, keep the back straight, and sink. This is a horse stance. Try to get your thighs parallel to the floor. Raise the arms above the head. Extend the arms with the palms of the hands facing upward to the sky. Sink at the waist and extend with the arms. Focus straight ahead. Breathe 9 times and lower in your stance with each breath until you are deep in the stance.

SHUAI CHIAO CHI GONG:

LEANING FORWARD TO SEARCH FOR THE SEA

Leaning Forward to Search For the Sea is a very challenging exercise. It works the calves, thighs, back, and arms. It is especially good for working balance. Stand on your right foot. Extend your left foot behind you. Extend your arms in front of your face. Touch the first finger and thumb of your right hand to the first finger and thumb of your left. This makes a diamond shape. Focus your gaze through the diamond. Now bend your right knee and drop. Extend your arms and your back leg for balance. Your goal is to get the thigh on your supporting leg parallel to the ground. Lean forward and search for the sea.

Once you have done this on one side, switch legs and work the other side.

SHUAI CHIAO CHI GONG:

SWALLOW SKIMS THE WATER

Swallow Skims the Water works on the thighs, the calves, the forearms, and the fingers. Place feet together. Bend at the knees and the hips. The lower you drop, the more your muscles will work. Make each hand into a crane's beak—your fingertips lightly touch the end of the thumb. Extend the arms behind you. Focus your eyes straight ahead. You should feel like you are tucked into a downhill skier's position. Quickly move your fingertips so they touch and release the thumb. Touch and release; touch and release. The faster you move your fingers, the harder the muscles in your forearms will work.

FORMS

Shaolin Northern Long Fist Kung Fu has many traditional forms that incorporate effective self-defense applications into them. By working the forms, one repeats these self-defense applications until they become second nature. The forms work on the principle of muscle memory. The more one uses a particular muscle, the quicker and stronger the muscle becomes. Form-work in the martial arts is an excellent tool for improving speed, timing, reflexes, power, strength, memory and overal fitness.

The martial arts are all about respect. In this picture, Mr. Toomer demonstrates a salutation form used to display courtesy at Karl Romain's Kung Fu Academy.

Amani Toomer, who is nicknamed THE GOAT by fellow teammates, "The Greatest Of All Time" and Sifu Karl Romain.

SAMPLE WORKOUTS

THIS IS JUST A SAMPLE OF THE TYPE OF WORKOUTS INCLUDED IN THE PROGRAM. TO FULLY APPRECIATE THE FULL RANGE OF CONDITIONING EXERCISES OFFERED IN THE SHAOLIN ATHLETE/KUNG FU CONDITIONING PROGRAM, VISIT ONE OF OUR TRAINING SESSIONS AT EDGEWATER KUNG FU IN EDGEWATER, NEW JERSEY.

SAMPLE WORKOUT 1

WARM UPS:
Jump Rope
High Knees
Calf Pump
Stretch Kicks
Leap Frogs

STRENGTH TRAINING:
Palm Hooks
Stance Routine
Fly Catchers

REFLEX / AGILITY:
Hubud
Eye Contact Drill

COOL DOWN / STRETCH:
Tai Chi-Chi Gong
Partner Floor Stretching

WARM UPS:
JUMP ROPE

Attributes:
Flexibility, Power, Balance and Control, Coordination, Speed, Agility/Mobility, Endurance/Stamina, Reaction Time.

Muscles targeted:
The entire body.

Instructions:
Jumping Rope is a great warm up exercise. It raises the heart rate and gets your muscles ready for the rest of the workout.

Picture one:
Sifu Romain demonstrates the use of a jump rope. Begin with the rope just behind the feet.

Picture two:
Raise the rope over the head.

Picture three:
As the rope descends toward the feet, jump over the rope.

Picture four:
Continue as before.

Warm Ups:
Jump Rope

WARM UPS:
HIGH KNEES

Attributes:
Strength/Power, Endurance/Stamina.

Muscles targeted:
The High Knees drill is good for stretching out the leg muscles and for circulating blood throughout the body at the beginning of a workout.

Instructions:
High Knees is similar to running in place. The difference being that with High Knees you intentionally focus on bringing the knees up to or beyond the waist before setting the foot back down on the floor. The knees should go up and down rapidly.

Picture One:
Mr. Toomer brings his knee up to his hand while running on his toes.

Picture Two:
Mr. Toomer works his way across the floor by bringing his knees to his hands.

Warm Ups:
High Knees

WARM UPS:
CALF PUMP

Attributes:
Flexibility, Power, Balance and Control, Coordination, Speed, Agility/Mobility, Endurance/Stamina.

Muscles targeted:
The entire body, especially the leg muscles and arm muscles.

Instructions:
Calf Pumps are another great warm up exercise. They raise the heart rate and get your muscles ready for the rest of the workout.

Picture One:
Sifu Romain demonstrates Calf Pumps. Begin in an attention stance.

Picture Two:
Pump your hands up toward the ceiling.

Picture Three:
As your hands go toward the ceiling, jump forward and land on toes. Continue moving forward down the floor.

Warm Ups:
Calf Pump

WARM UPS:
CALF PUMP

Instructions (continued):

Picture Four:
After you jump, bring your hands back to your side and land on your toes.

Picture Five:
After you land, pump your hands back up toward the ceiling and jump. Repeat several times.

Warm Ups:
Calf Pump
(continued)

WARM UPS:
STRETCH KICKS

Attributes:
Flexibility, Balance and Control, Coordination, Speed, Agility/Mobility, Endurance/Stamina.

Muscles targeted:
The leg muscles.

Picture One:
The Front Stretch Kick stretches the leg muscles and increases flexibility. Mr. Toomer begins with his feet together and his arms stretches out in an Iron Cross Stance. His eyes are focused on a spot in front of him about a foot above eye level. He swings his right leg forward and up. His goal is to touch his forehead with his toes.

Picture Two:
Once his leg is fully extended, Mr. Toomer snaps his leg back into place. The leg returns twice as fast as it was sent out.

Do this exercise with both legs. You can perform the Front Stretch Kick in one spot on the floor or by moving across the floor.

Warm Ups:
Stretch Kicks

WARM UPS:
LEAP FROGS

Attributes:
Flexibility, Power, Balance and Control, Coordination, Speed, Agility/Mobility, Endurance/Stamina.

Muscles targeted:
The entire body, especially the leg muscles, the back, and the core.

Instructions:

Picture One:
Sifu Romain demonstrates this exercise. Begin in a low squat with your feet shoulders width.

Picture Two:
Jump up in the air and extend the body with the arms reaching up to the ceiling. Move forward as you leap in the air.

Picture Three:
Drop back into a low squat. Repeat this exercise over and over.

Warm Ups:
Leap Frogs

STRENGTH TRAINING:
PALM HOOKS

Attributes:
Strength, Focus

Muscles:
Strengthens the arm and shoulder muscles. This technique is especially effective for strengthening the muscles in the forearm.

Instructions:
Picture One:
Begin with feet shoulders width in a Standing Horse Stance. Stretch out arms into an Iron Cross with the arms fully extended, the wrists are bent so that the finger-tips point toward the ceiling. The fingers should be pressed tightly together with the thumb tucked into the palm. This forms a Willow Leaf Palm. The wrists should be level with the ears and the arms pulled back so that the shoulder blades are pinched together. Keep this posture solid throughout the exercise.
Picture Two: Quickly bend wrists and have all the fingers of the hand touch the thumb forming a hook. When you do this, your forearm muscles will contract.
Picture Three: Extend the fingertips back toward the ceiling with the palms facing out forming a Willow Leaf Palm.

This exercise should be performed multiple times until you begin to feel a burn in your shoulders and forearms. Keep a solid stance. Do not rock back and forth and do not drop your arms.

STRENGTH TRAINING:
PALM HOOKS

STRENGTH TRAINING: PALM HOOKS

STRENGTH TRAINING:
STANCE ROUTINE

Attributes:
Power, Balance and Control, Endurance/Stamina, Strength.

Muscles targeted:
Builds strength in the legs and the core.

Instructions:
Miss Chelsea Kinnard is pictured in a variation of a stance routine that strengthens the legs and builds a solid foundation for footwork.

Picture One:
Horse Stance. Extend legs to beyond shoulder's width with toes pointing forward. Bend at knees and waist. Keep the back straight. Try to get the thighs parallel to the floor.

Picture Two:
Forward Stance. Back leg should be straight with the heel of the foot driven into the floor. Front knee is bent and the thigh should be parallel to the floor.

Picture Three:
Empty Stance. All the weight is placed on the back leg. Knee is bent to add support. No weight is on the front leg.

STRENGTH TRAINING:
STANCE ROUTINE

STRENGTH TRAINING:
STANCE ROUTINE (CONTINUED)

Picture Four:

Drop Stance. Back leg is bent parallel to the floor. Front leg is straight. Back is straight

Picture Five:

Forward Stance (Repeated).

Picture Six:

Horse Stance (Repeated).

Strength Training:
Stance routine (Continued)

STRENGTH TRAINING:
FLY CATCHERS

(The Fly Catchers should be performed as one continuous drill that strengthens the fingers, hands, forearms, and shoulders. When you have completed one circle, then the drill is finished.)

Attributes:
Strength, Focus.

Muscles:
Fingers, hand, and forearm.

Instructions:

Picture One: Begin in the standing horse stance with the feet separated shoulders width. Allow your arms to hang by your side and extend your fingers.

Picture Two:
Quickly bring your fingers together into a clenched fist.

Picture Three: Quickly shoot the fingers out from the fist until they are fully extended.
(Open and close the hands quickly five times)

As you repeat this exercise you will begin to feel the muscles in your hand start to burn. This exercise is excellent for strengthening the muscles of the hand and the forearm.

Strength Training:
Fly Catchers

STRENGTH TRAINING:
FLY CATCHERS (CONTINUED)

Instructions (continued):

Picture Four:
Next, stretch your arms out to the side and extend your fingers.

Picture Five:
Again, quickly bring your fingers together into a clenched fist.

Picture Six:
Quickly shoot the fingers out from the fist until they are fully extended.
(Open and close the hands quickly five times)

STRENGTH TRAINING:
FLY CATCHERS (CONTINUED)

STRENGTH TRAINING:
FLY CATCHERS (CONTINUED)

Instructions (continued):

Picture Seven:
Next, stretch your arms above your head and extend your fingers.

Picture Eight:
Again, quickly bring your fingers together into a clenched fist.

Picture Nine:
Quickly shoot the fingers out from the fist until they are fully extended.
(Open and close the hands quickly five times).

STRENGTH TRAINING:
FLY CATCHERS (CONTINUED)

STRENGTH TRAINING:
FLY CATCHERS (CONTINUED)

Instructions (continued):

Picture Ten:
Next, stretch your arms in front of your body and extend your fingers.

Picture Eleven:
Again, quickly bring your fingers together into a clenched fist.

Picture Twelve:
Quickly shoot the fingers out from the fist until they are fully extended.
(Open and close the hands quickly five times).

Strength Training:
Fly Catchers (Continued)

STRENGTH TRAINING:
FLY CATCHERS (CONTINUED)

Instructions (continued):

Bring your arms back to your side, that is the end of the first set. Continue to rep the cycle.

Strength Training:
Fly Catchers (Continued)

REFLEX/AGILITY TRAINING:
HUBUD

Attributes:
Coordination, Speed, Agility/Mobility, Focus, Sensitivity and Awareness, Reaction Time.

Muscles targeted:
Hand/eye coordination and the arms.

Instructions:
Hubud is a two-person drill that works on sensitivity, reflexes, speed, and focus. It works on a three movement pattern—deflect, push, and strike. When an opponent strikes, the defender deflects the attack, pushes the attack away (or redirects the attack), and strikes back.

Picture One:
Mr. Toomer throws a Willow Leaf Palm at Sifu Romain. Sifu Romain blocks the palm up and away. He parries the attack by pushing the arm away with his free hand.

Picture Two:
Sifu Romain pushes down on Mr. Toomer's arm.

Picture Three:
Sifu Romain throws a palm strike toward Mr. Toomer. Mr. Toomer parries the strike up and away.

Reflex/Agility Training:
Hubud

REFLEX/AGILITY TRAINING:
HUBUD (CONTINUED)

Instructions continued:

Picture Four:
Mr. Toomer deflects the attack, pushes it away, and strikes back. This attack and counter-attack exchange is great for building sensitivity and reflexes.

Picture Five:
The drill continues.

Picture Six:
The drill continues.

Reflex/Agility Training:
Hubud (Continued)

REFLEX/AGILITY TRAINING:
EYE CONTACT DRILL

Attributes:

Focus, Confidence, Sensitivity and Awareness.

Muscles targeted:

The Eyes.

Instructions:

Mr. Toomer throws a single punch toward Sifu Romain.
Sifu Romain softens his focus so that he sees the punch
and follows the punch without blinking or flinching.
This exercise works on focus. It also works on
Mr. Toomer's speed, timing, and control as he fires his
punch toward Sifu Romain.

Reflex/Agility Training:
Eye Contact Drill

Cool Down/Stretch:
Tai Chi—Chi Gong
Loosening the Neck

Flexibility.

Muscles targeted:

The neck muscles

Instructions:

Picture One:

Sifu Romain begins in a Standing Horse Posture with his muscles relaxed.

Picture Two:

Inhale as you slowly turn the head to the right and look over the right shoulder. This helps to relax the muscles. Do not strain the neck as you turn. Keep your muscles relaxed.

Picture Three:

Exhale as you return the head to the forward position.

Picture Four:

Inhale as you turn the head to the left and look over the left shoulder.

Picture Five:

Return the head to the forward position. Exhale.

COOL DOWN/STRETCH:
TAI CHI–CHI GONG
LOOSENING THE NECK

COOL DOWN/STRETCH:
TAI CHI—CHI GONG
RELAXING THE SHOULDERS

Attributes:

Flexibility.

Muscles targeted:

The shoulder muscles

Instructions:

Picture One:

Sifu Romain begins in a standing horse posture with his muscles relaxed.

Picture Two:

Inhale as you slowly roll the shoulders up and back allowing the hands to rise along your centerline.

Picture Three:

When you hands reach shoulder level, begin to exhale.

Picture Four:

As you exhale, pinch your shoulder blades together and allow the hands to separate.

Cool Down/Stretch:
Tai Chi—Chi Gong
Relaxing the Shoulders

COOL DOWN/STRETCH:
TAI CHI—CHI GONG
RELAXING THE SHOULDERS (CONTINUED)

Instructions:
Picture Five:
Inhale and begin to bring the hands together.

Picture Six:
Continue to inhale and bring hands together at your centerline.

Picture Seven:
Exhale and allow the hands to drop.

Picture Eight:
End the exercise with your hands by your sides.

COOL DOWN/STRETCH:
TAI CHI—CHI GONG
RELAXING THE SHOULDERS (CONTINUED)

COOL DOWN/STRETCH:
TAI CHI—CHI GONG
BOW, BEND, AND STRETCH

Attributes:
Flexibility.
Balance.

Muscles targeted:
Back muscles

Instructions:

Picture One:
Begin in a standing horse position with your hands at your sides.

Picture Two:
As you inhale, allow your hands to slide down your thighs.

Picture Three:
Continue to inhale and allow your hands to slide to your knees.

Picture Four:
Bend your knees and allow your hands to slide to the top of your feet.

Cool Down/Stretch:
Tai Chi–Chi Gong
Bow, Bend, and Stretch

COOL DOWN/STRETCH:
TAI CHI—CHI GONG
BOW, BEND, AND STRETCH (CONTINUED)

Instructions:

Picture Five:
Exhale and straighten your legs allowing your hands to slide to your knees.

Picture Six:
Continue to exhale and allow your hands to slide to your knees.

Picture Seven:
Bring your hands to your waist and slowly raise your head.

Picture Eight:
End the excercise in the standing horse position.

COOL DOWN/STRETCH:
TAI CHI—CHI GONG
BOW, BEND, AND STRETCH (CONTINUED)

COOL DOWN/STRETCH:
TAI CHI–CHI GONG
POLISHING THE MIRROR

Attributes:
Strength.
Balance.

Muscles targeted:
The shoulder muscles
The thigh muscles

Instructions:

Picture One:
Begin in a high horse stance with palms facing out.

Picture Two:
As you inhale, bring palms together and drop in your horse stance.

Picture Three:
Allow palms to descend down your centerline and continue to drop in your horse stance.

COOL DOWN/STRETCH:
TAI CHI—CHI GONG
POLISHING THE MIRROR

COOL DOWN/STRETCH:
TAI CHI—CHI GONG
POLISHING THE MIRROR (CONTINUED)

Instructions:

Picture Four:
Circle the palms outward and exhale.

Picture Five:
Continue to exhale, circle the palms out, and start rising in your stance.

Picture Six:
Exhale and rise in your stance with your palms facing out.

COOL DOWN/STRETCH:
TAI CHI—CHI GONG
POLISHING THE MIRROR (CONTINUED)

COOL DOWN/STRETCH:
TAI CHI—CHI GONG
STEPPING OVER THE FENCE

Attributes:
Flexibility.
Strength.
Balance.

Muscles targeted:
The leg muscles

Instructions:

Picture One:
Begin in a standing horse. Inhale and shift weight onto your left leg.

Picture Two:
Continue to inhale. Raise the right hand and the right knee.

Picture Three:
As you exhale imagine that you are gently stepping over a fence.

Cool Down/Stretch:
Tai Chi—Chi Gong
Stepping Over the Fence

COOL DOWN/STRETCH:
TAI CHI—CHI GONG
STEPPING OVER THE FENCE (CONTINUED)

Instructions:

Picture Four:
Continue to exhale and begin to lower your hand and foot.

Picture Five:
Allow your heel to touch the floor and shift the weight to the right.

Picture Six:
Come back to the standing horse position.

Cool Down/Stretch:
Tai Chi—Chi Gong
Stepping Over the Fence (Continued)

COOL DOWN/STRETCH:
TAI CHI—CHI GONG
WHITE STORK KICKS UP

Attributes:
Flexibility.
Strength.
Balance.

Muscles targeted:
The leg muscles

Instructions:

Picture One:
Begin with your feet together and your arms crossed in front of your chest. As you inhale, shift your weight to your right let.

Picture Two:
Continue to inhale. Open your arms so your palms face outward besides your ears. Bring the left leg up and begin to kick out.

Picture Three:
As you exhale, kick out and extend your arms.

COOL DOWN/STRETCH:
TAI CHI—CHI GONG
WHITE STORK KICKS UP

COOL DOWN/STRETCH:
TAI CHI—CHI GONG
WHITE STORK KICKS UP (CONTINUED)

Instructions:

Picture Four:
Allow your arms and your left leg to drop.

Picture Five:
Allow your left heel to touch the floor first.
Allow your arms to drop until they are crossed in front
of your chest. Bring feet together.

Now shift your weight to the left leg and kick out
with the right leg.

COOL DOWN/STRETCH:
TAI CHI—CHI GONG
WHITE STORK KICKS UP (CONTINUED)

COOL DOWN/STRETCH:
PARTNER STRETCHING

Attributes:

Flexibility

Muscles:

The leg and back muscles

Stretching is an important part of any workout. As you stretch, picture the muscles elongating. Remember to breath as you stretch. Stretch to the point of pain and then pull back. Stretching should create discomfort, but not pain.

Instructions:
Picture One:

Cynthia lies on her back, and Sifu Romain presses her knees down toward her chest cavity. Cynthia lets Sifu Romain know when to stop pressing.

Picture Two:

Sifu Romain continues to press Cynthia's knees toward the floor.

Picture Three:

Sifu Romain presses Cynthia's knee to her left allowing her back muscles to stretch.

COOL DOWN/STRETCH:
PARTNER STRETCHING

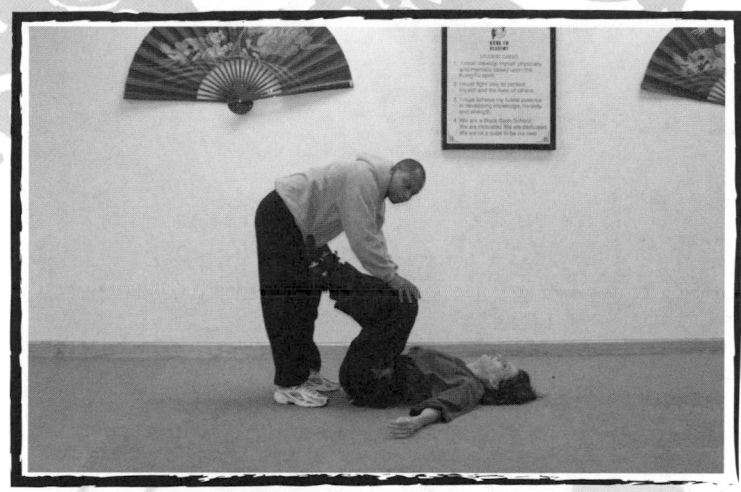

Cool Down/Stretch:
Partner Stretching (Continued)

Instructions (continued):

Picture Four:
Sifu Romain readjusts Cynthia's knee to the upright position.

Picture Five:
Sifu Romain presses Cynthia's right knee back toward her chest cavity while keeping her right leg straight. This concentrates the stretch on the left leg.

Picture Six:
Sifu Romain presses Cynthia's left leg to the floor while continuing to press her right knee into her torso. This intensifies the stretch. Notice that Sifu Romain keeps his hands on the knees to assure that no undue pressure is placed on the knee joint.

COOL DOWN/STRETCH:
PARTNER STRETCHING (CONTINUED)

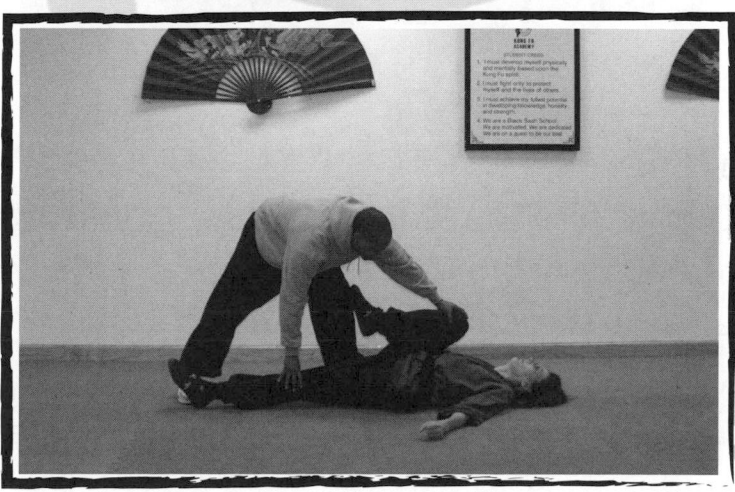

COOL DOWN/STRETCH:
PARTNER STRETCHING (CONTINUED)

Instructions (continued):

Picture Seven:
Sifu Romain straightens out Cynthia's left leg and presses back on it pushing it toward her head. This continues to intensify the stretch. Notice again that Sifu Romain has his hand on Cynthia's knee to make sure that the knee isn't injured during the stretch.

Picture Eight:
Sifu Romain continues to press Cynthia's leg toward her head. Cynthia lets Sifu Romain know when he should stop pressing.

Picture Nine:
When Cynthia tells Sifu Romain that he should release pressure, he slowly brings the leg back up and away from her face to the starting position.

COOL DOWN/STRETCH:
PARTNER STRETCHING (CONTINUED)

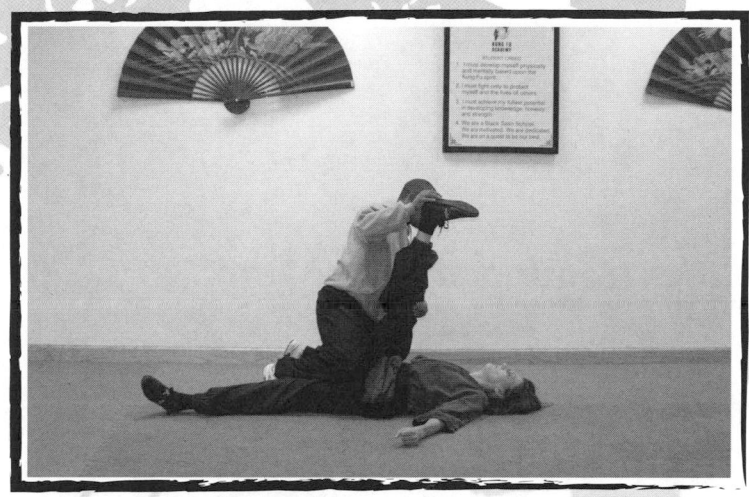

COOL DOWN/STRETCH:
PARTNER STRETCHING (CONTINUED)

Instructions (continued):

Picture Ten:
Sifu Romain begins the stretch for a second time.

Picture Eleven:
Sifu Romain continues the stretch until Cynthia asks him to stop.

Picture Twelve:
Notice how Sifu Romain continues to add support to Cynthia's knee during the stretch.

COOL DOWN/STRETCH:
PARTNER STRETCHING (CONTINUED)

COOL DOWN/STRETCH:
PARTNER STRETCHING (CONTINUED)

Instructions (continued):

Picture Thirteen:
Sifu Romain presses Cynthia's knee into her chest cavity.

Picture Fourteen:
Sifu Romain continues the press until Cynthia informs him that he should release the stretch.

Picture Fifteen:
Sifu Romain inititates the stretch for a second time.

COOL DOWN/STRETCH:
PARTNER STRETCHING (CONTINUED)

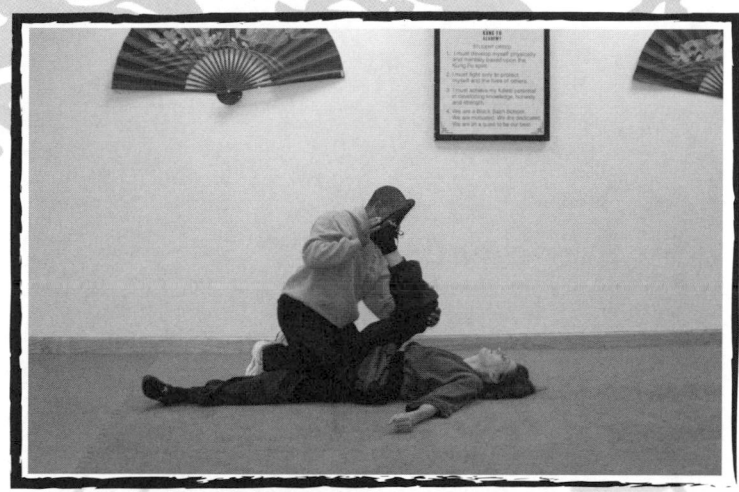

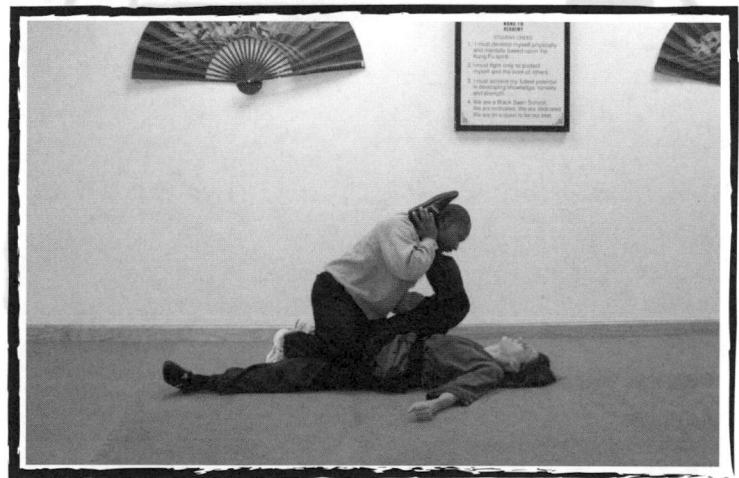

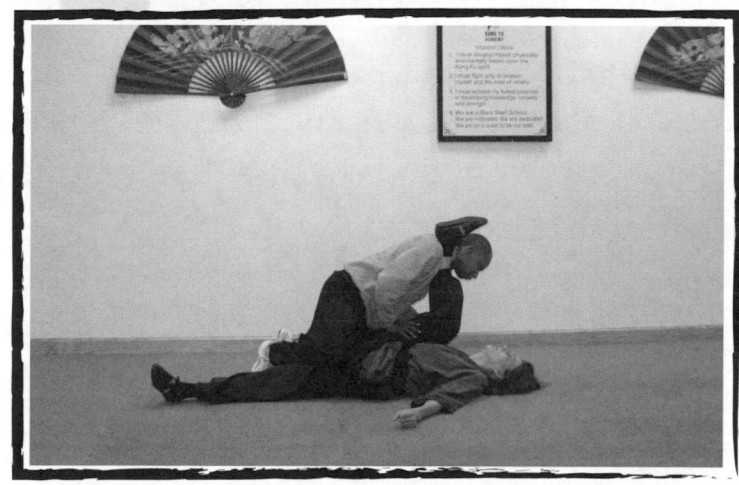

COOL DOWN/STRETCH:
PARTNER STRETCHING (CONTINUED)

Instructions (continued):

Picture Sixteen:
Sifu Romain relaxes the stretch.

Picture Seventeen:
Sifu Romain begins the stretch again. He pushes her right knee back and down.

Picture Eighteen:
Sifu Romain presses Cynthia's knee into her chest cavity, playing close attention to make sure that Cynthia is not in pain during the stretch.

COOL DOWN/STRETCH:
PARTNER STRETCHING (CONTINUED)

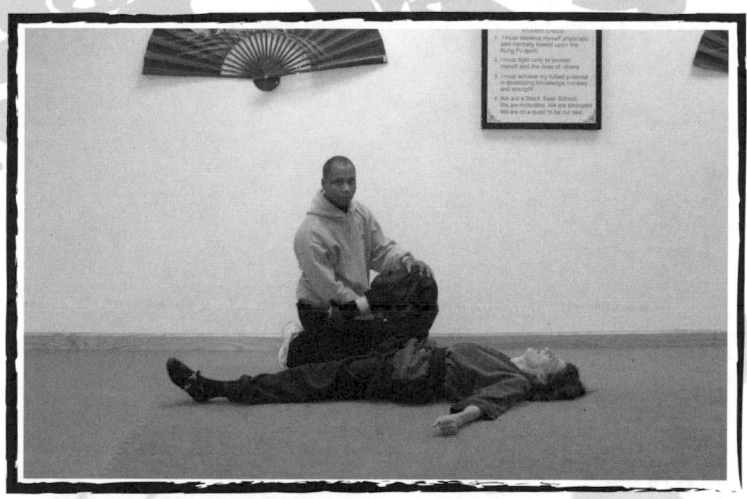

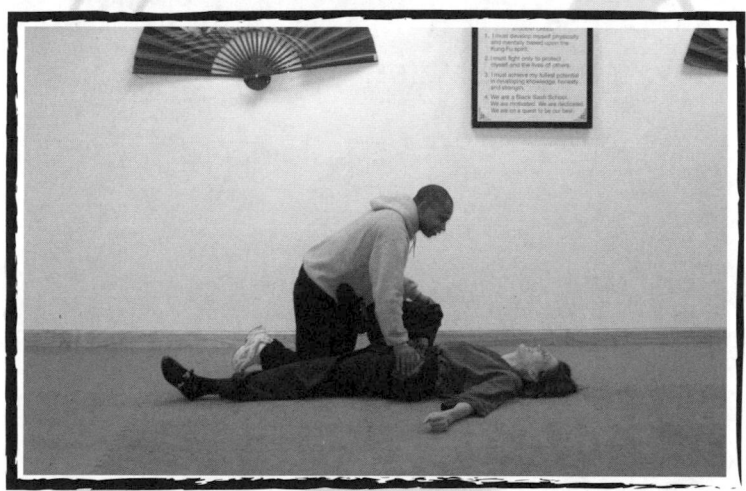

COOL DOWN/STRETCH:
PARTNER STRETCHING (CONTINUED)

Instructions (continued):

Picture Ninteen:
Sifu Romain presses the right knee to the left stretching Cynthia's lower back muscles.

Picture Twenty:
Sifu Romain continues the stretch.

Picture Twenty-one:
Sifu Romain continues the stretch until Cynthia asks him to release it.

Cool Down/Stretch:
Partner Stretching (Continued)

COOL DOWN/STRETCH:
PARTNER STRETCHING (CONTINUED)

Instructions (continued):

Picture Twenty-two:
Sifu Romain lifts the leg back to the right.

Picture Twenty-three:
Sifu Romain presses the knee back.

Picture Twenty-four:
Sifu Romain gathers both knees for a final stretch.

Cool Down/Stretch:
Partner Stretching (Continued)

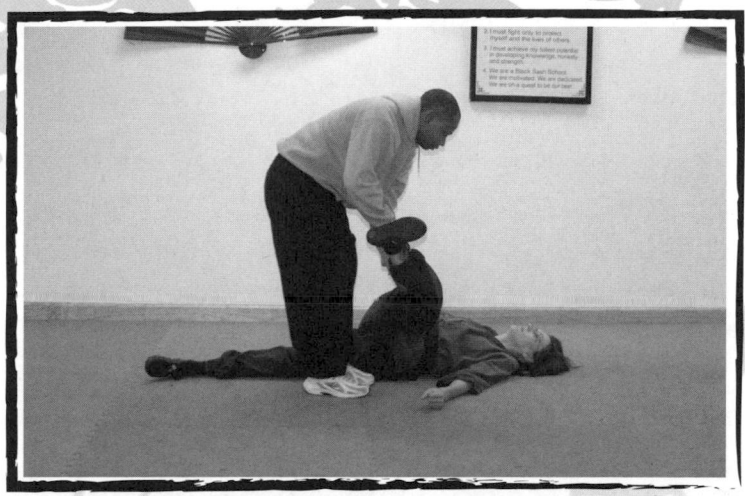

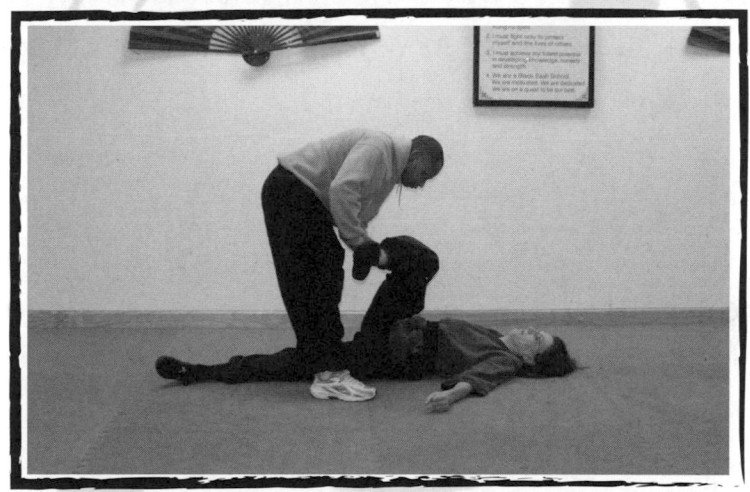

COOL DOWN/STRETCH:
PARTNER STRETCHING (CONTINUED)

Instructions (continued):

Picture Twenty-five:
Sifu Romain presses both knees back toward the chest cavity. This is the same as when the stretches began.

Picture Twenty-six:
Sifu Romain releases the tension.

Picture Twenty-seven:
Sifu Romain pushes back on the knees for one final stretch.

Cool Down/Stretch:
Partner Stretching (Continued)

SAMPLE WORKOUTS

SAMPLE WORKOUT 2

WARM UPS:
Jumping Jacks
Monks Punching Drill
Horse Stance Punching Drill

STRENGTH TRAINING:
Eagle Claw Push Ups
Shuai Chiao Chi Gongs
- Three Planes
- Sharpening the Ax
- Angel Staring in the Mirror
- Pointing to the Winner
- Combined Lying Stance
- Swallow Skims the Water
- Leaning Forward to Search for the Sea

REFLEX / AGILITY:
Push Hands

COOL DOWN / STRETCH:
Wall Stretch

WARM UPS:
JUMPING JACKS

Attributes:
Flexibility, Balance and Control, Coordination, Speed, Agility/Mobility, Endurance/Stamina.

Muscles targeted:
The entire body, especially the leg muscles and the arm muscles.

Instructions:
Jumping Jacks are another great warm up exercise. It raises the heart rate and gets your muscles ready for the rest of the workout.

Picture One:
Sifu Romain demonstrates Jumping Jacks. Begin in the Attention Stance.

Picture Two:
As you jump separate your feet and send your hands out and up.

Picture Three:
Allow your feet to land under your shoulders. The hands come together above the head.

Picture Four:
As you jump, bring your feet and hands back together into the Attention Stance. Repeat this exercise over and over.

Warm Ups:
Jumping Jacks

WARM UPS:
MONKS PUNCHING DRILL

Attributes:
Power, Balance and Control, Coordination, Speed, Agility/
Mobility, Strength, Endurance/Stamina, Reaction Time.

Muscles targeted:
Great cardiovascular workout. Also strengthens and builds
the legs, the core, and the arms. Works the total body.

Instructions:
Miss Chelsea Kinnard takes us through the basic moves
in the Shaolin Monks Punching Drill.
Picture One: Attention Stance.
Picture Two: Circle arms out to the side and then above
the head.
Picture Three: Hands come together above the head.
Keep hands together and lower them toward the chest.
Picture Four:
As you lower the hands toward the chest, you step out
with the left foot into a horse stance. This is the opening
posture for the Shaolin Monks Punching Drill.
Picture Five:
Left hand forms into a willow leaf palm. Send the palm
out from the body slowly tensing the muscles in the arm
as you send out the palm. Exhale as you send out the
palm from the body.
Picture Six:
Punch forward with the right arm while you stand on the
right leg. The left leg comes up to form a crane stance.
Exhale and say "Ha" as you punch.

Warm Ups:
Monks Punching Drill

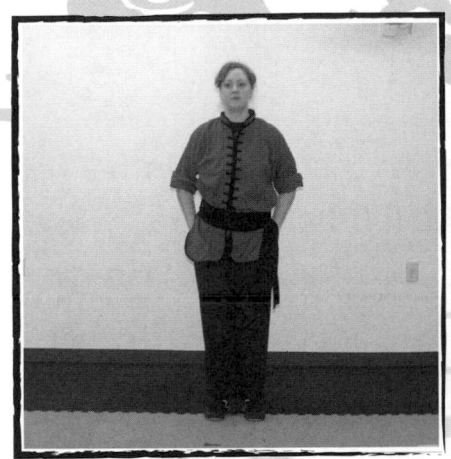 

WARM UPS:
MONKS PUNCHING DRILL (CONTINUED)

Instructions:

Picture Seven: Step down with the left leg into a horse stance. As you step down, the left hand forms a willow leaf palm and the right hand forms a fist. Smash the back of the fist into the palm.

Picture Eight: Punch forward with the left arm while you stand on the left leg. The right leg comes up to form a crane stance. Exhale and say "Ha" as you punch.

Picture Nine: Drop the right leg into a horse stance and punch out with the right hand. This is a short punch. Exhale and say "Ha" as you punch.

Picture Ten: Punch out with the left hand. This is also a short punch. Exhale and say "Ha" as you punch. Repeat this cycle of crane stances and punches three times.

Picture Eleven:
This begins the closing sequence. Hands circle out to the sides and then up above the head.

Picture Twelve:
When hands get above the head, put the palms together. Begin to lower the hands toward the chest.

Warm Ups:
Monks Punching Drill (Continued)

WARM UPS:
MONKS PUNCHING DRILL (CONTINUED)

Instructions:

Picture Thirteen:
With palms together lower hands to chest level. This concludes the Shaolin Monks Punching Drill.

Picture Fourteen:
Bring feet together and hands to the side. This is the Attention Stance.

Warm Ups:
Monks Punching Drill (Continued)

WARM UPS:
HORSE STANCE PUNCHING DRILL

Attributes:
Power, Coordination, Speed, Agility/Mobility, Endurance/Stamina, Focus, Confidence, Reaction Time.

Muscles targeted:
The legs, arms, and the core.

Instructions:
Picture One:
Sifu Romain drops into a horse stance with his right fist extended in front of his body. His left hand is in chamber.

Picture Two:
Sifu Romain punches out with his left hand. His right hand returns to chamber. His focus is on the valley between the first two knuckles of his fist. He punches out and hits the same spot with every punch.

Warm Ups:
Horse Stance Punching Drill

WARM UPS:
EAGLE CLAW PUSH UPS (FRONT VIEW)

Attributes:
Strength and Power, Endurance and Stamina.

Muscles:
Strengthens the fingers, arms, core, back, and legs.

Instructions:
Picture One:
Begin in the attention stance.

Picture Two:
Bend at the waist and place your fingertips on the floor. Using your fingertips, walk your hands out in front of your body until you are in a position to do a push up.

Picture Three:
Once you are in push up position, execute a fingertip push up.

Warm Ups:
Eagle Claw Push Ups (Front View)

WARM UPS:
EAGLE CLAW PUSH UPS (FRONT VIEW)

Instructions continued:

Picture Four:
Execute the fingertip pushup.

Picture FIve:
Walk the hands back to your feet by pushing back
with your fingertips.

Picture Six:
Rise up and stand in the Attention Stance.

Warm Ups:
Eagle Claw Push Ups (Front View)

WARM UPS:
EAGLE CLAW PUSH UPS (SIDE VIEW)

WARM UPS:
Eagle Claw Push Ups (Side View)

STRENGTH TRAINING:
SHUAI CHIAO CHI GONG

Shuai Chiao is Chinese Wrestling. Chi Gong literally means, "energy work" or "energy exercise." Shuai Chiao Chi Gong is a set of exercises that strengthens the body specifically for the art of Chinese wrestling.

THREE PLANES:

Attributes:
Power, Balance and Control, Strength/Power, Endurance/Stamina, Focus.

Muscles targeted:
Strengthens the thighs, calves, forearms, shoulders, and fingers.

Instructions:
Picture One and Picture Two:
Sifu Romain and Mr. Toomer demonstrate the posture used in Three Planes. Place the feet together. Bend at the knees and at the waist. Focus the eyes straight ahead. Bend the arms at the elbows and the wrists. Form the hands into a crane's beak with the fingertips lightly touching the thumbs. Quickly move the fingertips so they touch and release on the thumb. Touch and release; touch and release. The faster you move your fingers, the more you work the forearm muscles. The lower you drop in your stance, the more you work your thighs and calves.

Strength Training:
Shuai Chiao Chi Gong
Three Planes

STRENGTH TRAINING:
SHUAI CHIAO CHI GONG
SHARPENING THE AX

Attributes:

Power, Balance and Control, Strength/Power, Endurance/
Stamina, Focus.

Muscles targeted:
Strengthens the thighs, calves, forearms, shoulders, and
fingers.

Instructions:

Picture One and Picture Two:

Sifu Romain and Mr. Toomer demonstrate the posture
used in Sharpening the Ax. Place the feet slightly past
shoulder's width with the toes pointing forward. Drop
into a low horse stance. Extend the arms directly in front
of the chest and pull back on the wrists. The palms face
outward and the fingertips of each hand are held tightly
together. You will begin to feel a burning sensation in
your arms and your legs. The lower you drop, the more
your legs will burn.

Strength Training:
Shuai Chiao Chi Gong
Sharpening the Ax

STRENGTH TRAINING:
SHUAI CHIAO CHI GONG
ANGEL STARING IN THE MIRROR

Attributes:
Power, Balance and Control, Strength/Power, Endurance/
Stamina, Focus.

Muscles targeted:
 Strengthens the thighs, calves, core, back, forearms,
shoulders, and fingers.

Instructions:
Sifu Romain and Mr. Toomer are in the right forward
stance position. The back (left) leg is locked out and the
forward (right) leg is bent at the knee. Notice that the
right thigh is parallel to the floor. The lower you drop
into this stance, the more the leg muscles are challenged.
Both hands form a Crane's beak, meaning that the finger
tips lightly touch the end of the thumb. The right arm
extends to the back. The left arm bends at the elbow until
the hand is in front of the face. Focus on the fingers of
the left hand (this is the mirror). Quickly move the finger
tips so they touch and release on the thumb. Touch and
release; touch and release. The faster the fingers move;
the more the forearms work.

STRENGTH TRAINING:
SHUAI CHIAO CHI GONG
ANGEL STARING IN THE MIRROR

STRENGTH TRAINING:
SHUAI CHIAO CHI GONG
POINTING TO THE WINNER

Attributes:
Power, Balance and Control, Coordination, Strength/
Power, Endurance/Stamina, Focus.

Muscles targeted:
Strengthens the legs and arms.

Picture One:
Sifu Romain adjusts Mr. Toomer's arms. The arms are set
in a position to help Mr. Toomer envision that he is
holding a staff.

Picture Two:
Mr. Toomer is in the crane stance. He raises his right
foot off the floor and bends his leg at the knee. The left
knee of the supporting leg is also bent. The deeper you
drop into the stance, the more you work the leg muscles.
Mr. Toomer holds his right hand above his head and his
left hand is at his waist. His focus is straight ahead.

Once you complete this exercise on one side of the
body, switch legs and work the other side.

Strength Training:
Shuai Chiao Chi Gong
Pointing to the Winner

STRENGTH TRAINING:
SHUAI CHIAO CHI GONG
RHINO WATCHING THE MOON

Attributes:
Flexibility, Power, Balance and Control, Coordination, Strength/Power, Endurance/Stamina, Focus.

Muscles targeted:
Stretches the lower back and the leg muscles.

Rhino Watching the Moon works balance. It also stretches the back muscles, the calves, and the hamstrings. Mr. Toomer demonstrates the posture. Cross the feet—left foot over the right. Make the right hand into a fist. Bring the right hand to chamber or to your pocket. Bend at the waist. Stretch your left arm around to your right calf. Try to reach behind your right calf. Stretch. Envision your muscles elongating. Focus your eyes on your elevated elbow. You will have to fight to keep your balance. The more your bend and stretch; the more challenging this exercise becomes.

Once you complete this exercise on one side of the body, switch legs and work the other side.

Strength Training:
Shuai Chiao Chi Gong
Rhino Watching the Moon

STRENGTH TRAINING:
SHUAI CHIAO CHI GONG
COMBINED LYING STANCE

Attributes:
Flexibility, Power, Balance and Control, Strength/Power, Endurance/Stamina, Focus.

Muscles targeted:
Strengthens the legs, the back, and the arms.

Sifu Romain and Mr. Toomer demonstrate the Combined Lying Stance. Extend the feet out past the shoulders. Bend at the knees, keep the back straight, and sink the body toward the floor. Raise the arms above the head. Extend the arms with the palms of the hands facing upward to the sky. Breath in and out nine times dropping a little lower each time you exhale. On the ninth breath, you should be at your lowest position. Try to get your thighs parallel to the floor. Focus straight ahead. Hold this stance as long as possible. Begin by holding it for thirty seconds and build from there. You will begin to feel your legs and arms burning. Continue to challenge your body and your mind as you hold this stance.

Strength Training:
Shuai Chiao Chi Gong
Combined Lying Stance

STRENGTH TRAINING:
SHUAI CHIAO CHI GONG
SWALLOW SKIMS THE WATER

Attributes:
Flexibility, Power, Balance and Control, Strength/Power, Endurance/Stamina, Focus.

Muscles targeted:
Strengthens the legs, the back, the arms, and the hands.

Sifu Romain and Mr. Toomer demonstrate Swallow Skims the Water. Place the feet together. Bend at the knees and the waist. Lean the upper body forward. Make each hand into a Crane's Beak—your fingertips lightly touch the end of the thumb. Extend the arms behind you. Focus your eyes straight ahead. You should feel like you are tucked into the position of a downhill skier. Quickly move your fingertips so they touch and release on the thumb. Touch and release, touch and release. The faster you move your fingers, the more you work your forearm muscles. Challenge your mind and body by holding this stance until your muscles are fatigued.

Strength Training:
Shuai Chiao Chi Gong
Swallow Skims the Water

STRENGTH TRAINING:
SHUAI CHIAO CHI GONG
LEANING FORWARD TO SEARCH FOR THE SEA

Attributes:
Flexibility, Power, Balance and Control, Strength/Power, Endurance/Stamina, Focus.

Muscles targeted:
Strengthens the legs, the back, the core, the arms, and the hands.

Sifu Romain and Mr. Toomer demonstrate Leaning Forward to Search For the Sea. This is a very challenging exercise. Stand on your right foot. Extend your left foot behind you. Extend your arms in front of your face. Touch the first finger and the thumb of your right hand to the first finger and thumb of the left hand. This makes a diamond shape. Focus your gaze thorough the diamond. Now bend your right knee and drop. Extend your arms and your back leg for balance. Your goal is to get the thigh of your supporting leg parallel to the ground. Lean forward and search for the sea through the diamond formed by your hands.

Once you have performed this exercise on one side, switch legs and work the other side of the body.

STRENGTH TRAINING:
SHUAI CHIAO CHI GONG
LEANING FORWARD TO SEARCH FOR THE SEA

REFLEX/AGILITY:
PUSH HANDS

Attributes:
Balance and Control, Coordination, Sensitivity and Awareness.

Muscles targeted:
This drill builds sensitivity in the hands and arms. It strengthens muscles in the legs, the back, and the core. This drill also works Chi circulation throughout the body, which reduces stress and has other great health benefits.

Instructions:

Picture One:
Sifu Romain settles his weight on his back foot as Cynthia presses her arms forward. Sifu Romain places his open palms on Cynthia's elbows to keep her from advancing.

Picture Two:
Sifu Romain uses his right arm to lift Cynthia's arm. He circles her arm around, and he presses forward.

Picture Three:
Sifu Romain presses into a forward stance. Cynthia settles her weight onto her back foot and catches Sifu Romain's elbows with her palms.

Reflex/Agility:
Push Hands

REFLEX/AGILITY:
PUSH HANDS (CONTINUED)

Instructions:

Picture Four:
Cynthia takes a defensive posture with her weight settled into her back foot and her palms pressed against Sifu Romain's elbows.

Picture Five:
Cynthia uses her right arm to lift Sifu Romain's arm. She circles his arm around, and she presses forward.

Picture Six:
Cynthia presses into a forward stance. Sifu Romain settles his weight onto his back foot and stops Cynthia's elbows with his open palms.

REFLEX/AGILITY:
PUSH HANDS (CONTINUED)

COOL DOWN/STRETCH:
WALL STRETCH

Attributes:

Flexibility, Balance and Control.

Muscles targeted:

Stretches the leg and groin muscles creating long, lean flexible muscles.

Instructions:

Picture One:

Cynthia positions her body along the wall. She presses her back against the wall and stretches out her arms for balance. Notice the toes of her right foot are pointed toward the wall. Cynthia's right hand is on the floor for balance. Sifu Romain takes Cynthia's left leg and helps her prepare her mind for the stretch. It is extremely important that you relax your muscles and continue to breathe during the stretch. Imagine your muscles elongating and becoming more flexible.

Picture Two:

Sifu Romain begins to press Cynthia's leg up and back toward the wall.

Picture Three:

Sifu Romain continues to press Cynthia's leg up and back until her muscles are fully stretched. When stretching you should feel discomfort in the muscles, but not pain. When you start feeling pain, this is your body telling you to back off and relax.

COOL DOWN/STRETCH:
WALL STRETCH

KUNG FU BREATHING

Morihei Ueshiba writes of breathing, "Rise early in the morning to greet the sun. Breathe in and let yourself soar to the ends of the universe; breathe out and bring the cosmos back inside. Next breathe up all the fecundity and vibrancy of the earth. Finally, blend the Breath of Earth with that of your own, becoming the Breath of Life itself. Your body and mind will be gladdened, depression and heartache will dissipate, and you will be filled with gratitude."[15]

Breathing is an important part of our Kung Fu Conditioning program. In Kung Fu, we breathe through our nose with our tongues lightly touching the roofs of our mouths. We breathe deep into our lower abdomen just below the belly button in the *dantian*.[16] Our breathing should cause our stomach to push out on our sashes or belts.

Breathing helps you focus. It helps control your heart rate. When you focus on your breathing, it helps you take your mind off your pain. Pregnant women are taught breathing exercises to help with pain management during childbirth. When people get angry, they often are told to take some deep breaths and to count to ten. Martial artists have been using breathing exercises to manage pain and emotion for hundreds of years. Managing pain often comes down to mind over matter. Proper breathing can help with pain management. Every great athlete must learn to manage their pain and to control their emotions. Learning Kung Fu breathing techniques helps here.

As you train, practice proper breathing. As you breathe, focus on your breath. As you focus on your breath, you will find that you can strengthen your focus on whatever task is at hand.

A Note on Shuai-Chiao Postures

Jennifer Lawler in *The Martial Arts Encyclopedia* defines Shuai-Chiao by writing, "In China, the contemporary name for wrestling, though Chinese wrestling itself goes back nearly three thousand years. It resembles both Karate and Judo, for it uses both striking and grappling methods. It was similar to archery in importance to the classical warrior, and, exported to Japan, was a powerful influence on the development of Jujutsu."[17] Similar words include Shuai-Go, which Lawler defines as, "A style of Chinese wrestling popular during the Ming and Ching Dynasties", and Shuai-Jiao, which Lawler defines as "a Chinese term for physical training."[18]

PART III

The Shaolin Athlete's Mind and Spirit

If there is right in the soul,
there will be beauty in the person.
If there is beauty in the person,
there will be harmony in the home.
If there is harmony in the home,
there will be order in the nation.
If there is order in the nation,
there will be peace in the world.

—Lao Tze

CHAPTER ONE

SIFU KARL ROMAIN[19]—

MY JOURNEY IN THE MARTIAL WAY

"The Impossible Dream"
—Lyrics by Joe Darion

*To dream the impossible dream
To fight the unbeatable foe
To bear with unbearable sorrow
To run where the brave dare not go
To right the unrightable wrong
To love pure and chaste from afar
To try when your arms are too weary
To reach the unreachable star
This is my quest to follow that star
No matter how hopeless, no matter how far
To fight for the right, without question or pause
To be willing to march into hell
For that heavenly cause
And I know if I'll only be true
To this glorious quest*

That my heart will lie peaceful and calm
When I'm laid to my rest
And the world will be better for this
That one man scorned and covered with scars,
Still strove with his last ounce of courage
To reach the unreachable star. [20]

(Sifu Karl Romain) was born on September 24, 1967, in Port-au-Prince, Haiti. My parents, Claude and Louis Romain, moved our family to New York when I was two years old. Like so many parents who immigrated to America, my mom and dad were seeking a better life for us. They both worked to support our family. From an early age, they instilled within us the value of education and hard work. I am grateful for the opportunities my parents gave me when they decided to move to the United States.

I originally sought out Kung Fu training for the same reason that thousands of other people around the world began to train in Kung Fu—the influence of a man from Hong Kong named Bruce Lee. I have been studying and training in the martial arts for more than thirty years. My real Kung Fu training began at age ten. This is when I found my instructor, Mr. Reuben Prett. When I met my instructor, I thought, "I want to be just like him." Mr. Prett guided me in my Kung Fu journey for the next fourteen years—from a novice to a world champion. He encouraged me to train with my eye on the prize of the world championship. He also encouraged me to become an instructor in Kung Fu.

My Kung Fu training was very different than you find in most martial arts academies today. Located in Pearl River, New York, it was not a commercial school. To train there, you had to receive an invitation. The school did not have air conditioning in the summer or heat in the winter. You sparred without any sparring gear. Punches and kicks were real punches and kicks. Weapons training was with real weapons—real swords and real knives. The workouts lasted two hours. You went to class three days a week. If it sounds "old school," that's because it was. But I loved it. I would often walk several miles from my home in Nyack to the school in Pearl River to receive training.

I especially loved the philosophical overtones of Mr. Prett's training. He trained his students in the way of the *Wu Te*—the Martial Virtue. He taught the ideals of right and wrong. He expected his students to show respect and to be loyal. He trained his students not to misuse their skills. Mr. Prett taught his students how to avoid fights. He taught us more than just the skills of Kung Fu; he taught us how to live life. He taught us how to live the martial way. Mr. Prett expected all his students to learn about the Chinese culture—ancient China, modern China, the history, the people, the country, the terrain, the food, the clothing, the religion and philosophy. Training in Kung Fu was an education.

People sometimes ask me to compare the school where I trained growing up to the academies that I run today. But it is really unfair to make the comparison. They are different worlds. In the old schools they had the philosophy, "Many picked; few chosen." Today, each individual has the choice of working toward a black sash.[21] If you put in the time and effort, then you will progress to black sash. Martial arts schools today are professional schools where the staff is trained to run a business. Training today is a totally different experience. There are not as many injuries. You train with sparring gear on mat floors. Back then, the "tough guy" sought out training. Today parents enroll their children so they can learn life skills along with self-defense training.

In 1985, I attended my first martial arts tournament in Washington, DC. Dennis Brown hosted the tournament, and the biggest names in Kung Fu were there—Willie "The Bam" Johnson, Keith Hirabayashi, Richard Branden, and Cynthia Rothrock. At this tournament, I caught the fever to compete. Five years later, I would be world champion. After graduating from high school in 1986, I traveled to California to train. While in California, I trained with Eric Chen and Keith Hirabayashi. After three weeks, I came back to New York and took different jobs so that I could buy a car and pay the bills. As I was doing this, I continued to focus on tournament training. Later, I commuted to Boston and trained with Richard Branden. In Boston, I added to my training the extra components of weight training, running, visualization, and personal development.

In 1990, I entered the World Association of Kickboxing Organization's World Championship in Venice, Italy. I represented the United States in this international competition. I specialized in Shaolin Long Fist Kung Fu. The judges based their scoring on technical ability, stance work, speed, power, focus, flexibility, movement, and artistic expression. I was named the World Association of Kickboxing Organization's World Champion at this tournament. All of my training had now paid off. I was world champion.

Since my world championship in 1990, many students have sought me out to help them train to become world champions. My experience in competition has made me a valuable resource for those who are pursuing the dream of becoming a world champion. Here is a list of some the people whom I have trained who have competed and won the title of World Champion:

Three-time World Champions:

Malcolm Higgins	Austria 2001
	Italy 2002
Felicia Gorham	Austria 2001
	Italy 2001
Lee Weber	

World Champions:

Willard Szeto	Italy 2002
Dany Michelle Peavey	Ireland 2004
Kathryn Dowd	Ireland 2004
Amy K. Frugé	Switzerland 2005
Randall Frayser	Switzerland 2005
Sandra K. Geffert	Switzerland 2005
John Lu	2008 and 2010
Jodie Taylor	
Benjamin Polansky	
Meghan Polansky	
Brandon Colona	
Carolina Gonzales	
Zackery Morris	
Jack Abajian	
Duy Nguyen	
Torie Blakelock	
Kindall Taylor	
Nigel Scopelitis	
Andrew Lambert	
Meagan Breazeale	
Cassius Wilkinson	

Team World Championship:

Team Wushu:	Ireland 2004
Kathryn Dowd	
Amy Frugé	
Britteny Kirsh	
Erin Hess	
Morgan Fentenot	

I must say that with God's help, I have conquered the odds more than once in this life. In 1988, I was in a car accident while crossing the Tappan Zee Bridge linking Rockland and Westchester Counties in New York. I could have died in that accident, but God spared my life. The accident left me with a severely injured back. The doctors told me that I had misaligned vertebrae in my back. They added, "It is not likely that you will be able to practice the martial arts again." But I did not give up. With the help of my chiropractor, I have been able to continue practicing and teaching the martial arts.

I have learned many lessons about what it means to dream big. I have taught these lessons at schools and academies across the nation. I teach, "Dare to dream. Follow your dreams. Do whatever it takes to accomplish your dreams. Dream the impossible dream."

I consider myself first a teacher and then a martial arts instructor. Teaching is my gift. Martial arts is my subject matter. I want to reach children. I know what the martial arts can do for children. It can change them.

I am the owner and master instructor for Edgewater Kung Fu in Edgewater, New Jersey. I have earned many top-level achievements in the martial arts. I have won awards in more than 400 state, regional, national, and world martial arts tournaments in fighting, forms, and weapons competitions.

Some of my achievements include:

- 1990: I was the World Association of Kickboxing Organization's (WAKO) World Champion.

- 1996: I was awarded the distinction of being inducted into the United International Kung Fu Federation's Hall of Fame.

- 1998: I was inducted into the World Christian Martial Arts Hall of Fame.

- September 2000: While representing the United States, I won silver and bronze medals in the weapons and forms divisions, respectively, of the World Karate Associations' (WKA) World Championships.

- August 2001: Again on the United States team, I won a silver medal in the forms division in the WKA World Championships.

- I have trained many professional athletes and have served as a special trainer for the New York Giants football team.

Karl Romain's Kung Fu Academy

On December 26, 1991 I opened my first Kung Fu Academy in Nyack, New York. While I concentrated on teaching the external art of Kung Fu, I invited Sifu Linda Morrissey to teach the internal art of Tai Chi. Together we began to share our knowledge and enthusiasm of the ancient art of Kung Fu with students in Rockland County, New York. Within a span of four-and-one-half years, the school in Nyack had developed its first black sash graduating class. Since then, hundreds of people have gone on to receive their black sash in Kung Fu and in Tai Chi.

Over the years, I have trained thousands of students in the art of Kung Fu. I have also had the privilege of traveling around the United States, holding clinics and workshops for eager students of all ages. My school offers both group and individual classes. A tournament team represents the school in state, national, and international tournaments.

Sifu Romain's Teaching Philosophy

"A PERSON WITH A FINE AND PURE HEART WILL FIND HAPPINESS. THE ONLY CONCERN FOR PARENTS SHOULD BE TO BRING UP THEIR CHILDREN AS NOBLE HUMAN BEINGS. THAT IS SUFFICIENT."[22]
—Shinichi Suzuki, author of *Nurtured by Love*

I have been teaching the martial arts for close to 20 years. I have trained dozens of instructors. I currently have around 20 men and women coming to my STORM Team/CIT instructor training class.[23] Currently, I have 250 students attending classes at Edgewater Kung Fu. In addition, I teach individual and group lessons at martial arts schools all over the United States. One of my life goals is to train 100 martial arts instructors who can impart the ancient knowledge of Kung Fu to students around the country. I am deeply saddened when I see other instructors who have acquired a vast knowledge of the martial arts, yet are not teaching any longer. Their knowledge will die with them. I want to make sure that the knowledge that I have been given will be passed on from generation to generation.

People sometimes ask me what I expect out of the people that I am training to become instructors? My teaching philosophy is this: We train character first and ability second. I believe that ability comes over time. We shouldn't make physical ability the center of our focus in teaching. We should focus more on the student being a good person. We should focus on leadership skills. Over time, the ability to perform at a high level in the martial arts or in any sport will come. If a person doesn't have the character to stick with the training, then the ability will never be developed. What gets in most people's way? Anyone can throw a punch or a kick. To truly help people, we must help them improve their confidence. We must build their self-esteem. We must teach them to respect themselves and others. We must get them to learn self-control, because self-control is the master key to success. These are attributes that change character.

I base my teaching philosophy on the Suzuki talent-education method. Shinichi Suzuki was a violin teacher who influenced teachers and students around the world. Suzuki's method can be found in his book *Nurtured by Love*. Suzuki writes, "The motto of my alma mater, Nagoya Commercial School, was 'First character, then ability.' These words were inscribed on a tablet that hung in the lecture hall. This principle has been a light to my path all my life and is written on my heart. Fine scholars, artists, businessmen, and politicians alike succeed in their fields only if they are fine men. In order to succeed one must first be a person of fine character."[24] This slogan—first character, then ability—is what guides me as I teach classes and as I teach others how to teach.

I have done many television interviews over the years. In one interview I was asked, "Do you use your martial arts in everyday situations?" I answered the reporter like this: "I use my martial arts every single day. Not the self-defense aspects of the art. I have that ready if I'm ever called upon to use it. But the martial arts are much more than just self-defense. The martial arts teach confidence, respect, self-control, self-discipline, and many other personal skills that I use every single day of my life." This illustrates the concept of character first, ability second.

When I teach my classes, I focus on the individual. I ask myself, "Am I reaching this person? Am I helping this person accomplish what they need?" I want to meet them where they are and raise them to another level. Our subject matter is the martial arts. But through martial arts training we are teaching confidence, self-control, self-discipline, respect, virtue, integrity, perseverance and so many other life skills.

When students come to class, they are taking time away from their busy schedules to learn. They want to be taught. If they didn't want to learn, then they would not come to class. Each student should leave class inspired. To inspire students means to put spirit in them. Students should leave class better prepared to face the world that awaits them, from having spent time with me in my class. Suzuki writes, "It is in our power to educate all the children of the world to become a little better as people, a little happier. We have to work toward this."[25]

What should you look for in a martial arts teacher? I look for five qualities in a great teacher: They must look the part (appearance is very important), they must act the part, they must walk the walk, they must exhibit a passion for martial arts and a passion for success, and they must maintain a positive mental attitude. These ingredients embody a great martial arts instructor. It is of vital importance that you as a student find a great teacher. One of the most important decisions that you will ever make as a martial arts student is the selection of your teacher. Some people search for years before they settle on the teacher that is right for them. Not all teachers are equal. Not all martial arts academies are equal. You must take the time in research, looking for the right teacher and the right school for you.

I believe that a great martial arts academy begins with patient and caring instructors. The academy must be made up of great people. You can have a great system, but if you don't have the right instructors to nurture and inspire people, then the school will not succeed. The way the information is passed on is important. How are the classes structured? Are the classes safe? Also, students should have tools to supplement their instruction. They should have DVDs and videos, so they can review material outside of class. A great martial arts academy cares about people. The academy wants its students to succeed in life and in the martial arts.

I have been a martial arts instructor for over two decades. I teach the martial arts because the martial arts have given me so much in life. Jesus taught, "Freely you have received, freely give." I love giving back to people through teaching the martial arts. But every time I give in my teaching, I find that I keep receiving back as much or more than I give. Teaching keeps me in touch with the students. Teaching helps me appreciate what I've learned over the years. Teaching reinforces my art and makes it better. I love teaching the martial arts.

When we teach, we have the power to influence and shape other people's lives. But if we teach skills without teaching heart and character, then what have we really accomplished? Remember the adage: "Character first, ability second." This teaching philosophy will help students to become better people. Teaching students to become better people is what teaching the martial arts is all about.

CHAPTER TWO

LESSONS IN THE MARTIAL WAY

Training is the psychological and physiological conditioning of an individual preparing for intense neural and muscular reaction. It implies discipline of the mind and power and endurance of the body. It means skill. It is all these things working together in harmony. [26]
—Bruce Lee, martial artist and film star

He who learns but does not think, is lost.
 He who thinks but does not learn is in great danger.
—Confucius

To be a great athlete takes much more than just physical conditioning. There is a mental side to athletics. The mental side is just as important as the physical side. In fact, the mental side often sets the elite athlete apart from the rest of the competition. Kung Fu Conditioning trains the mind as well as the body. It emphasizes the harmony of body, mind, and spirit.

The Shaolin athlete wants to improve as a person. This is a holistic approach to conditioning. By focusing on the following topics, you can grow mentally, emotionally, socially, and spiritually. These topics will harmonize your body, mind, spirit, and emotions. This will help you become the best athlete that you can be. It will also help you to become the best person that you can become.

1. Finding Your Voice

In Rockland County, New York, the local paper is *The Journal News*. This paper ran an obituary for a man who changed the world for all of us. The man who died is a person that I'm sure few if any of us had ever met, but surely all of us have enjoyed the benefits of his brilliant, scientific mind and his spirit of invention. Television watchers everywhere owe a great debt to this man of genius. The opening line of his obituary read, "Hit the mute button for a moment of silence: The co-inventor of the TV remote, Robert Adler, has died." The rest of the article read, "But he downplayed his role when asked if he felt his invention helped raise a new generation of couch potatoes. 'People ask me all the time—Don't you feel guilty for it? And I say that's ridiculous,' he said. 'It seems reasonable to control the TV from where you normally sit and watch television.'… His wife, Ingrid, said Adler wouldn't have chosen the remote control as his favorite invention. In fact, he didn't even watch much television. 'He was more of a reader,' she said. 'He was a man who would dream in the night and wake up and say—I just solved a problem. He was always thinking science.'"[27]

Robert Adler found his voice. He knew what he was good at doing. He was an inventor. So he invented things. One of his inventions just happened to be the TV remote.

Who is the greatest quarterback in football right now? Some would say Eli Manning. Others would argue that it is Aaron Rodgers. Now, imagine if Manning or Rodgers stopped playing football without any explanation. Many people would question their decision. Why? Because Eli Manning and Aaron Rodgers are two of the best quarterbacks in the game. Giants fans and Packer fans would be incensed. Each of these two men has found his voice. When you find your voice, people expect you to use it.

Once you find your voice and you use it, then you feel a sense of confidence and satisfaction that motivates you to develop that gift even more. You not only feel good about yourself, but you also motivate others and inspire them to find their voice. You do this, not with words, but by modeling change in your own life. You are giving back. And it is rewarding to give back.

Discovering Your Gift

What is my gift? To discover your gift ask yourself, "What is my unique, personal, and significant gift to the world?"

Unique: in that the gift belongs to you

Personal: in that the gift is yours to give

Significant: in that the gift can make a difference in someone's life

Contribution: in that the gift is something that you voluntarily give

Stephen R. Covey in his *The 8th Habit: From Effectiveness to Greatness* writes about four ways to discover your voice: talent, passion, conscience, and need.[28] I would like to think about three of these as we attempt to discover our voice: talent, passion, and need.

A. Talent.

Your talent is your natural, God-given strengths and abilities that are unique to you as an individual. Ask yourself: What am I good at? It might be motivating others, leading people, administration, or technology.

It is good to ask someone else what they see your natural abilities as being. You might think that your natural gift is singing, but if you are the only person who thinks that, then you need to rethink it. You might think that you are an encouraging person, but if you find yourself alone in a crowded room, then you might not be that encouraging.

B. Passion.

What excites you? What are you energized to do? What do you do without anyone else prompting you to do it? Is there anything that you get lost in doing? Time seems to fly by when you are doing this? Is there anything that you do that brings you a feeling of satisfaction?

Our passion and our talent should mesh. They should go together like chocolate and peanut butter or like milk and cookies. It is great to be passionate about something, but passion needs talent to be effective.

C. Need.

Once your recognize your talent and your passion, ask yourself, what need can be met with this gift? Does your voice allow you to provide for your family? Do other people appreciate your voice? Can you give back to society with your gift? Can your gift be used for the betterment of humanity? Are you able to create a personal legacy with your voice?

Once you find your voice, decide that you are going to use it to the best of your ability. Decide what legacy you wish to leave behind after you are gone. Then explore your voice and discover how your voice can create your legacy.

Joshua Chamberlain was a schoolteacher from the state of Maine, when he was called to serve in the Union Army in the Civil War. He was put in charge of a small company of soldiers. He wasn't a professional soldier, but he was a leader. When you are asked to lead, what do you do? You step up and lead.

During the Battle of Gettysburg, Chamberlain's company was given the order to hold the left flank of the Union line at all cost. Chamberlain understood the order. He was prepared to sacrifice his own life and the lives of his men to hold a small hill named Little Round Top.

On the second day of the battle, Confederate General Robert E. Lee ordered his men to take Little Round Top. Men from Alabama and Louisiana began marching up the hill, firing their rifles at Chamberlain's men. Chamberlain sent someone for help, but help never arrived. Chamberlain realized that he and his men were going to have to hold their ground on their own.

In the Civil War, the army that held the high ground had a distinct advantage. Chamberlain used that advantage to hold off the Confederate soldiers as long as he could. But as evening approached, Chamberlain's men were running out of ammunition. Chamberlain realized that once the ammunition was gone, the Confederate soldiers would overrun his position. So Chamberlain ordered his men to fix bayonets on their rifles. Then, without any bullets left in their rifles, Chamberlain gave the order, "Charge!"

He ordered his men to leave the security of the high ground, without ammunition, and to charge into the Confederate line. This took the Confederate soldiers by surprise. When they saw the Union soldiers charging down the hillside, the Confederate soldiers placed their rifles on the ground and surrendered. Chamberlain had held his ground.

This small victory on the second day of the Battle of Gettysburg helped turn the tide of the war. Had Lee gained the higher ground, then his artillery could have pounded the Union position. But thanks to the courage and leadership of Joshua Chamberlain, Lee was unable to gain the higher ground. The Union Army could now move their artillery up and pound Lee's army.

Joshua Chamberlain wasn't a professional soldier. But he was a leader. And he used his voice to change the tide in the Civil War and gain an important victory for Abraham Lincoln's army. Joshua Chamberlain used his voice, and now his legacy of leadership lives on in the annals of military history.

2. Goal Setting

"If you aim at nothing, you'll hit it every time."
—A leadership maxim

"If you don't know where you are going, you will probably wind up somewhere else." [29]
—Dr. Laurence J. Peter

When we wake up each day, we should say to ourselves, "This is the first day of the rest of my life. I am going to take charge and be in control today." Then we should ask ourselves, "What do I want to accomplish today?" If we begin each day with enormous goals, then we will end each day with enormous results. This section will guide you through some simple steps to help you accomplish your goals. But you must ask yourself, "Am I willing to live to my fullest potential?" As an athlete, are you willing to work to reach your fullest potential? Stop living in mediocrity and start living abundantly. Now is the time to see yourself at the highest level of your game.

First we must realize how important it is to set goals. A very low percentage of people have life goals. Those that do rarely hit those goals. This keeps people from realizing their full potential. As an athlete, it will keep you from your full potential. A research study sponsored by the Ford Foundation discovered that:

- 23 percent of the population has no idea what they want from life, and as a result, they do not have much.
- 67 percent of the population has a general idea of what they want, but they do not have any plans for how to get it.
- Only 10 percent of the population has specific, well-defined goals, but even then, seven out of the ten of those people reach their goals only half the time.

- The top 3 percent, however, achieved their goals 89 percent of the time.
- An astonishing 90 percent of the population has no ideas or plans for what they want out of life. [30]

Studies show that when you focus on your goals, you reach them 51% of the time. If we only reach just over half our goals when we are focused on them, imagine what happens when we don't focus on our goals. What happens? You accomplish nothing. As an athlete, you have to know what you want to accomplish. Set your goal, and then go achieve that goal.

Tackle your dreams and jump-start your desire to achieve your goals. By following a few practical guidelines, you will achieve your fullest potential as an athlete. Stop making excuses and begin to elevate your skills for a better tomorrow.

The Purpose of Goals

Why do we set goals? We set goals because we want to be successful. Goals point us toward success. Imagine yourself in much greater physical condition than you are right now. How much better could you play your sport in that condition? How much faster would you be? How much more endurance would you have? How much stronger would you be? You must set goals to reach this new level of conditioning.

Are you prepared to play your sport at the highest level? Are you ready to face the opposing player? We often hear, "Practice makes perfect." That's not exactly true. Perfect practice makes perfect. Better yet, perfect practice based on perfect planning makes an athlete perfect. This is the goal of *The Shaolin Athlete*—to help you reach your fullest potential as an athlete. But let's also realize that perfection is not a destination, but a state of constant progress.

Goal Setting 101

How do we set goals? Here is a simple formula:
PARR =
PLAN, ACT, REVIEW, RENEW.
Let's break it down and take a closer look at this four-step formula.

1. **PLAN.** Think of what you wish to accomplish. Evaluate what it

will take for you to accomplish this goal. Write down clearly definable goals and record your plan to reach that goal.

2. **ACT.** Carry out your plan. Act on what you have decided to do. Don't delay in carrying out your plan.

3. **REVIEW.** After you act on your goal, review the results. Get feedback from coaches and teammates. Feedback is the breakfast of champions, and it will chart your progress. When you review your progress and accept constructive criticism from your coach, then you will be able to target your weaknesses and enhance your strengths. Reviewing the goal tells you what changes you need to make as you get ready to set new goals.

4. **RENEW.** After you have reviewed the results of your action, then renew the goal. You might need to abandon the old goal altogether. You might need to tweak a particular part of the goal. Or, the goal might be just right for you. If so, reset the goal and give yourself a new deadline. Be persistent. Goals keep you going when you may otherwise give up. Renew your commitment to achieving your goals and keep pursuing your dreams. Overcome any obstacles to reach your goals. To continue when others give up is what sets the elite athlete apart from the average athlete.

Remember:

> As soon as you achieve your goal, set a new one.
> Always keep moving in the right direction.
> Goals give you hope.
> Hope gives you motivation.
> Motivation gives you energy—it excites you.
> Energy will help you achieve your ultimate goal.

The components of your goals should be motivated by your desire to leave a legacy and to benefit others. Prioritize your goals and begin with the most important. Organize your time and energy to reflect your priorities. Develop a proactive mindset.

Set your goals for the next five years. By age (fill in the age) I would like to accomplish or achieve (fill in the goal). In three to five years, you should start to see the results of your goals. Do not waste time. There must be a sense of urgency. A goal is a dream with a deadline. A shallow vision will yield empty results. Daniel H. Burnham, who left a menial job to form a company that helped to rebuild Chicago after the great fire of 1871, said, "Make no little plans, for they have no magic to stir men's blood." Do your best. Excel. Don't fall in the pit of mediocrity. Mediocrity results in failure. Steer clear of goals that are easily accomplished. Begin now.

How to Achieve Success Through Goal Setting

"People don't plan to fail, they fail to plan."

—a leadership maxim

1. Acknowledge the goal. Remember: The goals we set are the goals we get. Goals give us direction and keep us focused.
2. Acknowledge the benefits of the goal.
3. Acknowledge the obstacles in the way of the goal. Obstacles are what you see when you take your eyes off the goal. Obstacles are the enemy of goals. Obstacles come in many forms. Your response to obstacles can create more obstacles—distractions, fears, hesitation, a weak mind, loss of focus, and a defeatist attitude.
4. Secure necessary resources to accomplish the goal.
5. Acknowledge skills needed to accomplish the goal. You can't tailor-make the situations of life to accomplish the goal. But you can tailor-make the attitude needed to accomplish the goal. Begin with an attitude that is set for success.
6. Set a timeline for your goal. Time gets wasted when there is not a sense of urgency. Remember: A goal is a dream with a deadline.
7. Map out a written plan.
8. Take action. Logic will not always change an emotion but action will. Use your personal power and ability to take action.
9. Review your goals and your progress on a daily basis.
10. *Kachi.* Enjoy the victory. Celebrate the victory. The Japanese word for this is *Kachi.* When you reach a goal, take time to celebrate your accomplishment. After running a marathon, wear the medallion around your neck for the next few days. Bask in the glory of victory.

The Three Components Needed to Reach Your Goals:
> Belief
> Proper State of Mind
> Action

Four Excuses For Not Reaching Your Goals:
> Poor self-image
> Fear of not succeeding
> Not understanding how to establish goals
> Not believing in the importance of goals

Four Questions to Ask Yourself:
> What do I desire to be?
> What kind of life do I want to lead?
> Am I heading in the right direction?
> Will this action support my goals?

Questions to Ask Yourself Before the Season Opens:
> What is my ultimate goal for this season?
> What physical and mental abilities do I need to train to achieve my goal?
> > • Strength
> > • Speed
> > • Confidence
> What abilities do I need to work on the most?
> What must I do off the field this week to develop these abilities?
> What will I do at my next practice to develop these abilities?

3. Visualization

"Imagination is more important than knowledge."
—Albert Einstein

"Visualization is the key to higher self-esteem."
—Sifu Karl Romain

"A vivid mental picture if worth a thousand words." [31]
—James E. Loehr, sports trainer

What will it take to become a champion? First, you must see yourself as a champion. You have to see yourself holding the trophy as the best in your sport. Seeing in your mind's eye what you want to accomplish is the process of visualization.

Anything that has been created, was created twice. It was first created in the mind. It was visualized. Then it was created in the physical world. Visualization is a key ingredient in the creation process. Stephen R. Covey writes, "The first creation, vision, is the beginning of the process of reinventing oneself or of an organization reinventing itself. It represents desire, dreams, hopes, goals, and plans." [32]

Visualization doesn't happen without vision. You have to be able to see where you want to go. Without vision, people perish. Your vision will allow you to focus on your destination instead of your obstacles. It will allow you to see where you want to go and show you how to get there.

To be a success, you have to begin by visualizing your success. If you can't see it, then it won't happen. But when you can see it, then you can achieve it. Whatever you focus on in life, you become. If you see yourself as a winner, then you will become a winner. You will achieve what you set your mind to accomplish. Anything the mind of man is able to conceive, man is able to achieve.

One of the most important concepts in athletics today is visualization. Athletes are taught to visualize crushing a golf ball down the middle of the fairway, hitting a baseball over the centerfield fence, or catching a football for the game-winning touchdown. You see basketball players standing at the free throw line visualizing the ball going through the hoop. When you visualize something, you paint a picture of that event in your mind. You see yourself accomplishing the task before it happens. Martial artists have been using visualization for hundreds of years.

When I (Sifu Romain) participated in the Martial Arts World Championship Tournament, it was like an out-of-body experience. I had gone over my program so many times in my mind that I visualized doing it perfectly every single time. I did so much that when I went on the floor it was like I was watching myself as I was doing it.

When you visualize something, the mind cannot tell the difference between something that is imagined and something that is real. If you visualize something with emotion, you can make it seem real. James E. Loehr states this as a key point in his book, *Toughness Training for Life*, writing, "Your central nervous system can't tell the difference between something vividly imagined and something that actually happened."[33]

A study was performed to show the importance of visualization. One group of athletes practiced without any visualization techniques. Another test group used only visualization techniques and did not practice. A third group practiced and used visualization techniques. Obviously, the group that practiced and used visualization techniques performed the best and grew the most. But what proved interesting between the other two test groups was that the group that only used visualization techniques performed better than the group that practiced but did not use visualization techniques. That is the power of our gift of imagination. That is the power of visualization.

Another study was performed with violin students to see how visualization helped them learn to play music. Brain sensors were used to measure which parts of their brains were stimulated as they learned new pieces of music. The studies demonstrated that the exact same parts of the brain were stimulated when the violin student visualized playing the violin as when the student actually played the violin. To the human brain, visualizing something is as real as physically experiencing it.

The movie, *The Sphere*, displays the importance of the imagination and the magnitude of visualization in our lives. In the movie, all of the characters are affected by an outside source that causes their dreams to become real. Toward the end of the movie, Samuel Jackson's character comments, "The gift of imagination is the greatest gift in the world." If we recognize how wonderful the gift of imagination is, then we can use it to empower our lives and make us the best that we can be.

To practice visualization takes deliberate action. You have to take the time to focus on what you want to accomplish. You have to stop what you are doing and visualize where you want to go and what you want to be. You have to condition your mind toward visualization.

Kung Fu Conditioning teaches visualization. We often start our sessions with meditation. This is a time where we can clear our minds and focus on what we want to achieve in the training session. We use a calming breath to slow down our heart rate. We visualize ourselves doing our best.

Visualization is a huge part of martial arts training. Have you ever seen any of the old Kung Fu movies? What happens in those movies? In a movie like *Tai Chi Master*, Jet Li prepares to defeat his opponent by specifically visualizing the weaknesses of his opponent so that he can exploit those weaknesses. In doing this, he has already won the fight in his mind. And what we can conceive in our minds, we can achieve in real life.

When a martial artist practices a block or kicks the air or punches a bag, he or she is picturing in the mind doing the same against an opponent. Remember at the end of the first *Karate Kid* movie, Ralph Machio's character stands on one leg holding the crane stance with his arms outstretched like an iron cross. This is a stance that he had practiced hour after hour, day after day, while standing on the top of a pole. No one in the audience knew what he was doing. His opponent didn't know what he was doing. But he knew what he was doing. He was visualizing the one kick he needed to land on his opponent that would win the tournament. As his opponent approached, he landed the kick and won the tournament. What we can conceive in our minds, we can achieve in our lives.

Four distinct aspects of visualization:

A. One aspect of visualization is foresight. By foresight, we do not mean some psychic ability to predict the future. We do mean your ability to see what you want your future to be. A person with vision shapes the future while making the most of the present. You have to learn how to see the big picture. Stephen R. Covey writes, "Memory is past. It is finite. Vision is future. It is infinite. Vision is greater than history, greater than baggage, greater than the emotional scars of the past."[34] Visualization includes begin able to see what you want your future to look like. Then you go out and create your future.

B. Another aspect of visualization is the idea of knowing your voice. Do you know what you are meant to be in life? We are all born with a piece of music inside of us. You don't want to die without learning how to play that piece of music. When you find what you are meant to do in life, that's like playing the music. It is a bit of heaven on earth. Find what you are meant to be and make the most out of it. This is how to develop vision for your life. Visualization comes easier for those who can confidently affirm that they are doing what they are meant to do with their lives. They have found their gift. They have found their voice.

C. Another aspect of visualization is problem solving. The Chinese character that is translated as *crisis* has within it the symbol for opportunity. A visionary person doesn't just see the problems. He or she also sees the solutions. The visionary athlete looks for ways to improve on every situation. You must learn to see things, not as they are, but as you want them to be. This enables you to shape the future.

D. Another aspect of visualization is the idea of doing your personal best. Often, our idea of success is defeating the competition. We have to play better than the person who is guarding us. But this brings all the focus onto the opponent. Your focus needs to be on doing your personal best. What do Muhammad Ali, Michael Jordan, Tiger Woods, Jerry Rice, and Wayne Gretzky have in common? They all won several championships and set many records. But also, they were so far ahead of their competition that they had to focus on being their personal best. Jordan wasn't worried about outplaying an opponent. He could outplay anyone. He had to focus on doing his personal best every time out. Do you have enough vision to see what your personal best is?

One of the most important areas that we can spend time visualizing is in the area of our own personal development into a mature, successful person who lives life with confidence and gusto. See yourself as a person worthy of honor. See yourself receiving awards for your humanitarianism and your benefit to society. Look at yourself with respect. If you don't respect yourself, then why should anyone else show you respect? Visualize yourself as the person you want to be. Now go out and live up to that vision.

4. Self-Discipline

"Self-discipline is the master key to success."
—Sifu Karl Romain

"Only the disciplined are truly free."
—Stephen R. Covey

Visualization is an important ingredient in becoming a successful person. But visualization must be followed by self-discipline. You can sit around the house all day visualizing yourself at a ceremony receiving the Most Fit Person in Human History award; but if you don't get off your comfy chair and do some jumping jacks, pushups, and crunches, you're only dreaming. Your visualization will only become a reality if you have the discipline to act upon your vision. Discipline brings your dreams into reality.

Do you have the ability to do whatever is necessary to make yourself a better person without someone looking over your shoulder? That is self-discipline. Self-discipline is about character. Self-discipline is about doing what you need to do whether you like doing it or not. In order to succeed, you have to make yourself do the things you know you need to do whether you want to do them or not. And that is exactly what self-discipline is. Here is a great definition: **Self-discipline is doing the things you need to do, when you need to do them, whether you want to do them or not.**

Self-discipline is the bridge between thought and accomplishment. Self-discipline is forced behavior until that behavior becomes automatic. Self-discipline is doing what I know I should do without anyone reminding me to do it. Self-discipline is doing what I need to do whether I like it or not. Self-discipline is doing what needs to be done when it needs to be done.

Self-discipline propels the marathon runner to run an eighteen-mile practice run in the pouring rain. Self-discipline prompts the football player to go on the field in full pads when the thermometer says it is over 100 degrees on the field. Self-discipline drives the diver back up the ladder to the platform for one more dive because the last one was not up to standard.

In athletics, people hate repetition, but they envy success. You cannot succeed without repetition. You will not love repetition until you develop self-discipline. As a Shaolin Athlete, you will learn to love repetition. Sifu Romain has every student learn this maxim:

> Repetition is the mother of skill.
> The more you do it, the better you get.
> The better you get, the more confidence you have.

You must fall in love with the process. You might as well love the process, because as long as you are an athlete, you will be in the process.

Why do people fail? People fail because they are unwilling to do what they need to do to succeed. They don't want to work hard. They don't want to practice hard. They aren't willing to push themselves. You must keep saying to yourself, "I will persist until I succeed." This is the attitude of a self-disciplined person.

How Can I Improve My Self-discipline?

A. To improve self-discipline you must maintain an organized schedule. As noted earlier in the text, "People don't plan to fail; they fail to plan." Plan a daily training schedule. Stick to it. Sticking to a daily schedule injects self-discipline into life. This is a way of setting up personal accountability.

B. Another way to improve self-discipline is by maintaining a daily checklist. Zig Ziglar suggests that just before you go to bed, you list a few items that you want to get done on the next day. Don't write down too many items. Somewhere between three to six items is usually a good number. Sleep with that list under your pillow. Then when you get up the next morning, review the list and get going checking items off the list.

C. Kung Fu Conditioning increases one's self-discipline. Our training in the martial arts is all about self-discipline. As you push through the training, you are teaching yourself self-discipline. Just showing up for a training session is a matter of self-discipline. After you get through the warm-up and your body is hurting and your muscles are aching, do you have enough self-discipline to keep going? If you keep pushing through the pain and discomfort, then you are teaching yourself self-discipline. Sometimes this comes down to mind over matter. There is a toughness principle that applies here. We live in a society that has gotten soft. As Shaolin Athletes, we live by a different standard than most people. Most people run from hard work. The Shaolin Athlete runs toward hard work. We run toward hard work because we want to be our best. Self-discipline keeps us working at our goals until the desired result is achieved.

Remember: Winners do things that losers just aren't willing to do.

5. Passion

Under pressure, the mentally tough are passionate. By generating great emotion they are able to resist intense force from their competition. This capacity—the ability to summon high levels of positive emotional strength under the most stressful circumstances—is the trademark of the consummate competitor. [35]

—James E. Loehr, sports trainer

To achieve any goal takes vision. But, as we have seen, vision without discipline is just a daydream. Vision with discipline is the formula for success. Now take vision and discipline, and add a third ingredient to the mixture—passion. A person with vision, discipline, and passion is unstoppable. Champions are made with this formula. Stephen R. Covey writes, "*Passion* is the fire, the desire, the strength of conviction and the drive that sustains the discipline to achieve the vision."[36] Passion is the difference between mediocrity and excellence.

You can achieve anything if your passion for that achievement is strong enough. Passion is a by-product of inspiration. When you are inspired about something, it creates passion. The word *inspiration* means "to put spirit into someone." Inspiration breathes passion into our hearts. When you are inspired, you put your heart, soul, and emotion into it whatever you are doing.

But sometimes it is difficult to stay inspired. Therefore, our passion begins to wane. Playing sports can be like the process of falling in love. People fall in love, out of love, and back in love (and sometimes all of this happens on the same day). Because sports are so tough—tough on the body, mind, spirit, and emotions— you will fall in and out of love with your sport on a regular basis.

As a kid, you fell in love with your sport and you had big dreams about playing on a collegiate or professional level. Then you make it big. All of a sudden—*BAM!*— now there is all this pressure to perform. You lose focus on why you are there. You lose passion for the game.

In those moments, you need to rediscover your purpose and remind yourself of why you are playing your sport. If you are a professional athlete, wake up and smell the coffee! Realize that you are in a place that hundreds if not thousands of people would love to be. You are a part of an elite group of people who get to live out their dream on a daily basis. Renew your zeal and enthusiasm. Recommit yourself to your game.

When you find your purpose, then you perform at a different level. Just as passion is a by-product of inspiration, it is also a by-product of purpose. The athlete who knows his or her purpose is a passionate athlete. This person is a *Shaolin Athlete.*

A Test of Your Passion

A. Here is a quick test to see if you have passion for what you are doing. Ask yourself, would I work just as hard at this task, put in just as much energy and emotion, if no one were watching me? A passionate person doesn't need supervision. They give their all because they are passionate about what they are doing. They are intrinsically motivated to do their best because they love what they are doing. There is no longer any need for extrinsic motivation. Bret Favre, former quarterback for the Green Bay Packers, is quoted as saying, "I get paid to practice during the week. I play the games on Sunday for free." He feels that way because he is passionate about the game.

B. Here is another test: Ask yourself, do I get lost in this task? In other words, when you are engaged in this task, do hours fly by like minutes and minutes fly by like seconds? When you are truly passionate about something, you get lost in it. You forget about everything else because nothing else really matters. You are enveloped by your passion. I've seen people play golf during a hurricane. Why? Were they stupid? Some would say so. But real golfers don't care what others think about them. These golfers wanted to test the wind. They wanted to hit the ball with the wind at their back and see if they could drive the ball to the green on a 600-yard par five. If successful, they would hold the bragging rights on that hole for the rest of their lives (or until the next hurricane came through town). Some would call that stupid. For a true golfer, that's passion.

6. Focus and Concentration

What is focus? Sifu Romain defines focus as, "Applying yourself to a single task." Focus is setting your mind on something that you want to accomplish. You must prepare your mind in order to focus.

What is the difference between focus and concentration? Concentration is thinking through what you are told to do. Concentration is the thought process. Focus is the application of concentration. Think of concentration as the broader concept and within that concept is the idea of focus. In art, you have the broad brushstrokes of paint on canvas and then you have the fine details of pen and ink. Concentration is like the brush strokes, and focus is the pen and ink.

When we learn the art of single-minded focus, we gain great power. Most people don't know how to focus. Their mind rambles from one task to the next without ever giving their full attention to a single task. Athletes who learn how to focus on a single task will succeed in their sport. They will be team leaders. They will accomplish their goals. We teach our students, "What you focus on in life, you get." We also stress, "What you focus on in life, you become." One goal of Kung Fu Conditioning is to make you a more focused person. The Shaolin Athlete is a focused athlete.

Someone has said that people can be divided into three different groups: People who make things happen, people who watch things happen and people who say, "What happened?" The people who make things happen are the people who know how to focus. They center in on a specific task until that task is completed.

Life is full of distractions. If we allow distractions to steal our focus, then we will live distracted lives. The average person can hold his or her focus for no longer than two minutes at a time. This is a scary idea, but it is true. Most people have a very short attention span. If we can only hold our attention on a task for two minutes at a time, how do we ever accomplish anything? We must constantly refocus on the task at hand.

How long can you hold your focus? Try this exercise. Close your eyes and focus on your breathing. Count every breath. When you get to ten, go back and start over at number one. One to ten. One to ten. How long can you do this without getting distracted and without losing count? The average person will lose count very quickly. Serious athletes must be able to focus longer than the average person.

Two Important Concepts on Focus

A. Decide Where to Place Your Focus.

Where you place your focus is just as important as having the proper focus. Management studies have shown that in most corporations, 80% of the results come from 20% of the people. So if you are in a management situation, you need to focus on the right people.

Our focus will be pulled in many different directions. We must constantly refocus our attention, and make sure that we are focusing on the right thing. If we focus on the wrong area, then we won't make progress toward our goal and frustration will set in. We must make sure that our energy is expended in the right area to get the desired results.

Place your focus where it needs to be placed. If you are hammering a nail, you don't focus on the hammer. You focus on the nail. If you focus on the hammer, you'll find yourself refocusing on a smashed finger. Where we place our focus is of vital importance.

B. Finishing What You Start.

Focus means that when we start a task, we will see it through to completion. Prioritize your focus. Finish what you start. Don't start a new project until you complete the one that you are working on. When you start a new project, set a realistic goal of when you want the project completed. Work toward that goal. Don't get sidetracked by other projects. Finish what you start.

Kung Fu Conditioning and Focus

When you come to a Kung Fu Conditioning session, come focused. Without proper focus, your training will be fruitless. When you center your minds on a single task and give your full attention to that task, this is focus. We must apply this to our Kung Fu Conditioning exercises. While you are training, ask yourself, "How am I doing right now?" Focus deepens your training, and training deepens your focus. For example, when you sink down into a Shuai-Chiao posture, you need to focus on that posture and nothing else. When you punch a focus mitt, focus on the point of contact and punch like you were in a real life-or-death situation. Set your mind on the fist hitting the target in the exact spot where you plan for it to land. When you bring focus to your training, you get more from your training. You also walk out of training as a more focused person.

7. Mentors

One of the most important decisions that you will ever make as an athlete is the choice of your mentor or coach. Your mentor should not only prepare you for athletic competition, but a true mentor will help prepare you for life. Finding the right mentor is the key to being a champion. I (Sifu Romain) would never have even thought of becoming a world champion had my mentor not put the idea in my head. Once he planted the seed in my mind, he watered it, he nurtured it, and he caused it to grow. I owe my world championship to my mentor.

What Qualities and Attributes Should You Look for in a Mentor?

First and foremost, a positive mental attitude. You want someone who is going to inspire you and bring the best out of you. Life, the media, and your opponent will create enough negative energy in your life. Your mentor should feed you positive energy. This doesn't mean that he or she won't be critical at times and won't give negative feedback at times. Remember: Feedback is the breakfast of champions. But the criticism should always come with a healthy dose of positive reinforcement and positive feedback.

What is their life experience? Don't just look for someone who is knowledgeable about the subject area, but look for someone who has experienced life and has overcome challenges. You need someone who can provide a roadmap, which details not only the high points, but also the pitfalls to be avoided in life. A mentor's role is to guide the apprentice. The mentor doesn't want the apprentice to make the same mistakes that he or she once made.

Honesty and integrity. You should be able to trust your mentor. When you share something with your mentor, it should stay between the two of you. Without trust, you will not be able to entrust yourself to his or her direction.

Knowledge. Do they have a deep knowledge of the material they are sharing? How well do they know the subject matter? What type of experience do they have sharing their knowledge with students who want to learn? Who have they worked with? Where did they get their knowledge?

Ability. Can they do what they are telling you to do? Remember the ancient proverb, "To know and not to do is not yet to know." Bodhidarma, the person credited with initiating Kung Fu Conditioning at the Shaolin Temple in the Hunan Province of China, said it this way: "All know the way; few actually walk it." You want to find someone who walks the walk. You want a proven mentor who knows and lives what he or she is talking about.

A wise, loyal advisor. He or she is not there to be your friend. They serve as a guide to life.

How do you respond to a mentor?

Be a perfect student. Abandon your preconceptions and come saying, "I am ready to learn." Be an empty tablet. Be a sponge, ready to soak up whatever is taught. Approach your mentor like a beginning student. Clear your mind and be eager to learn. Shunryu Suzuki in *Zen Mind, Beginner's Mind* writes, "If your mind is empty, it is always ready for anything; it is always open to everything. In the beginner's mind there are many possibilities; in the expert's mind, there are few."[37] Approach your mentor like you are a beginner who has so much yet to learn.

Decide that you are going to be open with your mentor. Talk to your mentor about your challenges and your limitations. You must be able to trust your mentor to the point that you are brutally honest with him or her. A good mentor will call you out. A good mentor will challenge your weaknesses. He or she will set a standard that will cause you to raise your game. You must come ready to be challenged.

Once you find a mentor, don't question him or her. Just say, "Yes sir!" or "Yes ma'am!" The real wisdom in a mentoring relationship is to shut up and listen. Lao Tzu, the ancient Daoist philosopher said, " What is more malleable is always superior over that which is immovable."

Appreciate and value everything your mentor does. Give yourself wholeheartedly to your mentor.

The Eight Keys to Being the Perfect Student

The more skillful that one becomes (in the martial arts, for example), the more important it becomes to return continuously to the perspective of the beginner. That is the only way to resist the hegemony of entrenched habits and prevent becoming enslaved by one's own polished techniques. [38]
—Michael L. Raposa, author of *Meditation and the Martial Arts*

1. Respect your teacher/coach/mentor.
2. Trust your teacher/coach/mentor.
3. Keep an open mind.
4. Keep a "Yes, I Can" attitude.
5. Be responsible. Never fail to complete an assigned task.
6. Show your mentor your appreciation. Value what you are taught.
7. Give them your loyalty.
8. Always give back. Remember, givers get.

Never share your ideas or goals with people who do not support you. Clear out the dream-killers and surround yourself with people who encourage you to meet your goals. Surround yourself with positive people who are in agreement with your vision of the future. Find a mentor who is going to call you higher. They should challenge you to be your best. They should help you reach your full potential.

8. In Order To Grow, You Gotta Let Go: Overcoming Defeats and Setbacks

Life is growth. If we stop growing, technically and spiritually, we are as good as dead. [39]

—Morihei Ueshiba, founder of Aikido

Life isn't just about victories. It is also about defeats. For every mountaintop experience that we have, there is also a valley that we must cross to get to the next mountaintop. In life, how we handle our defeats is just as important as how we celebrate our victories.

I [Dr. Kinnard] remember lessons I learned while playing intramural football in college. During my sophomore year, the team I played on never won a game. In fact, we went the entire season without scoring a single touchdown. That year, we hung our heads in shame. After the losing season, we questioned whether we should play again the next year. Maybe we should focus solely on basketball or on baseball. But we didn't quit. We decided to work harder and to recruit some new talent for the next season. Even though we lost every game that season, we weren't losers. You can lose without being a loser. It's all in your attitude.

The next year, we did a little better, but we still had a losing record. I broke my leg during that season. I was running the ball toward the goal line when a linebacker jumped in front of me and got in position to make his tackle. I tried to make a move on him and fake him out when I should have ducked my head and barreled through him. I got hit high from one side and low from the other side. I heard my left tibia snap. I looked at the ref and said, "I just broke my leg. Can you get someone to carry me off the field?" He looked back at me and said, "Get up Kinnard; your leg isn't broken." I convinced him that it was broken and some players came and carted me off the field. The doctors at the emergency room confirmed that my leg was broken, and I had to wear a cast for eight weeks. After that season, I had doubts about playing my senior year. I would have to train extra hard to get over the disappointment of the last two seasons.

During my senior year, the whole team rallied together. We practiced harder. We listened to our coach and allowed him to coach us. We played together as a team. That third season, my senior year, we won the intramural championship and had a great celebration. We went from the team that everyone looked forward to playing because it was an easy victory and a way to run up their statistics, to the team that no one wanted to play. Although we lost some games, we weren't losers.

To be a winner, you can't have a defeatist attitude. You can't see yourself as a loser. You must use your defeats as stepping-stones to future victories. Think about the lessons that can be learned from defeats. Look at these teachings from great athletes and coaches:

> *Defeat is also a state of mind; no one is ever defeated until defeat has been accepted as a reality. To me, defeat in anything is merely temporary, and its punishment is but an urge for me to apply greater effort to achieve my goal. Defeat simply tells me that something is wrong in my doing; it is a path leading to success and truth.*[40]
> —Bruce Lee, martial artist and film star

> *I have missed more than 9,000 shots in my career. I have lost almost 300 games. On 26 occasions I have been entrusted to take the game winning shot… and missed. And I have failed over and over and over again in my life. And that is why… I succeed.*[41]
> —Michael Jordan, former NBA star

> *Success is never permanent, and failure is never final.*[42]
> —Mike Ditka, Super Bowl winning coach

> *One learns most about an athlete's mental toughness by observing how quickly he or she bounces back from emotional hits—missing free throws, double-faulting on break points, fumbling a touchdown pass. Watch the truly great competitors when they're losing or playing badly. They can take an emotional hit—lots of hits—and be right back in your face, hammering at your weak points, forcing you to make mistakes.*[43]
> —James E. Loehr, sports trainer

Remember the old adage, "If at first you don't succeed; try, try, again." No champion ever became a champion without overcoming defeats. Peyton Manning lost several playoff games before he went on to win the Super Bowl. Abraham Lincoln lost several elections before he won the big one—the election that made him the President of the United States of America (and arguably the best president this country has ever known). We are all going to face losses both in life and in sports. The question is not if we will lose; the question is, what we will do after we lose? Will we give up? Will we take on a loser's attitude? Or, will we learn from our defeats, train to never make the same mistakes again, and go out and play with the heart of a champion?

Beware of these reactions to loss or failure:

Lack of focus

Desire to quit

Burnout

Drop in confidence

Choking response (tendency to keep losing)

Lack of motivation

Not giving 100%

Tentative play

A broken spirit

Sometimes you need to get out of your own way to experience victory. We can be our own worst enemy. The idea is not about being perfect. It is about the pursuit of perfection and being the best we can be. Change the way you think about failure. See defeat as a lesson learned. Allow your mistakes, your failures, and your setbacks to be your best teacher. Wisdom is the application of experience.

When you lose, you can't take on a defeatist attitude. You have to be able to learn lessons from the defeat, but then put the loss in the past. Remember what we said at the beginning of this lesson, "In order to grow, you gotta let go." To grow, we have to let go of our past. This is true of past losses in sports, and it is true of past defeats in our lives. Here are some helpful tips to help you let go of the past:

1. We have to label *trash* as trash. When you hear tapes playing in your head that say things like, "You aren't good enough," "You'll never do better than this" or, "You are a loser. You were born a loser; you are a loser now; you'll die as a loser," these tapes have to be destroyed.

Label trash as trash. This takes self-examination. You might need help seeing the trash. Sometimes we can live with trash so long that we don't even see it. We get use to its smell. This is very true of negativity. We don't realize how negative we are. Don't be afraid to ask for help. A fellow athlete can help. Your mentor can help. A family member or a close friend might be able to help. Sometimes all you need is a sounding board to bounce ideas off. At other times you might need to see a therapist who can help you go deeper into your psyche to see what you are saying to yourself. You have to be able to see the trash in your life and label it as trash.

2. You have to empty the trash. Once you identify what is trash, you have to empty that trash. Every Monday and Wednesday in my (Dr. Kinnard's) neighborhood, the trash collectors come and haul away the trash. That means that every Sunday night and every Tuesday night, we set our trash cans out by the side of the street. Every Monday night we set out recycling. What happens if we don't set out the trash? The trash collectors won't collect it, and it starts building up. We are only allowed to place two trash cans by the side of the street. And it is amazing how quickly they can fill up. You have to empty those trash cans or you get a bigger problem—trash on top of trash with no place to put it. You have to empty the trash.

Do you know what trash talk is? Trash talk is when you bad mouth your opponent and tell him or her that she isn't quick enough or strong enough or talented enough or tough enough to beat you. You get in their head and make them feel like they have already lost. Why do so many athletes talk trash? Why? Because it works. People say that Michael Jordan was great at getting in the opponent's head. But that's because the opponent allowed him to get there. Label the trash talk as trash and throw it away.

We need to throw away whatever gets in our way. Dee Hock, founder of Visa International, says, "The problem is never how to get new, innovative thoughts into your mind, but how to get the old ones out."[44] Taking out the trash is a tedious, troublesome chore. I don't know many people who like to do it. But if we don't empty the trash, then it starts to overflow. It can eventually take over our lives if it remains unchecked. Label the trash, and then empty the garbage.

3. You have to choose to grow. Growth is a choice. Change begins with a decision. You have to press forward to better days ahead. You can choose to shape your future by learning from the past and by making great use of the present. We don't have to be victims. We don't have to have a defeatist attitude. You can reinvent yourself every day. Stephen Covey, author of *The Seven Habits of Highly Effective People* was asked if he really believed that people could live by the seven habits.

He said it was possible, but that it was more difficult at the beginning trying to learn how to live by the habits. He compared it to a rocket that was trying to get to the moon. The toughest part of getting a rocket to the moon is achieving lift-off and escaping the earth's gravitational force. Once the rocket has passed out of the earth's gravity, then the rocket can achieve orbit around the earth or the moon and basically float in space. But to get to the floating, it takes much energy and work. The same is true in life. To get to the floating, it takes much work. *In order to grow, you gotta let go.*

What are some reasons why people don't let go of the past?

A. Because it's familiar. It's their comfort zone. They have been labeled as a loser, and the label has stuck. Losing doesn't make you a loser. Not if you grow and change from your losses. Whatever happened in your past doesn't make you a loser. Not if you use the past to make you a better person.

B. Because they are embarrassed. They are embarrassed by their mistakes, so they don't want to admit them. This would mean coming clean and that would be an embarrassment. So they act like they are okay, like they don't have anything to change, but they are lying to themselves and to everyone else.

C. Because they don't believe they can change. They've been this way too long. It is too much to ask. They've tried to change before and have failed. Therefore, they can't change.

But, in order to grow, you gotta let go. Change always begins with a decision. You might say:

I want to lose ten pounds; therefore, I decide to exercise and eat right.

I want to make better grades; therefore, I'll pay better attention at school and study harder.

I want to connect with my child or with my parent; therefore, I will do my best to build the relationship and show love and respect for this person.

Change starts with a decision.

You can change. Change is possible. George Lucas did a great job making the *Star Wars* movies. The first three are the best. They happen to be episodes 4–6. In episodes 1–3, you see Anakin Skywalker become Darth Vader. In 4–6, you see Darth Vader become Anakin Skywalker. Darth Vader changed. He gave up the dark side and changed. Change is possible. In order to grow, you gotta let go. Label the garbage. Empty the trash. Set your sights high and decide that you will be a different person.

In order to grow, you gotta let go. Let go and start growing.

Consider one of Bruce Lee's favorite motivational poems. It is found in the book, *Bruce Lee: Artist of Life*.[45]

The Man Who Thinks He Can
by Walter D. Wintle

If you think you are beaten, you are.

If you think you dare not, you don't.

If you like to win, but think you can't

It is almost certain you won't.

If you think you will lose, you are lost.

For out of the world we find

Success BEGINS with a fellow's WILL.

It's all in the state of mind.

If you think you're outclassed, you are.

You've got to think high to rise.

You've got to be sure of yourself before

You can ever win a prize.

Life's battles don't always go to

The stronger or faster man.

But sooner or later the man

Who wins is the man

WHO THINKS HE CAN!

9. Repetition

The obvious answer to all things is practice and more practice. The more you practice, the more the "spirit of the thing itself" will reveal itself to you. [46]
—from the *Martial Artist's Book of Five Rings*

Almost nothing in the martial arts is possible without repetition." [47]
—from Suino's *Art of Strength, Art of Serenity*

We are what we repeatedly do:
Watch your thoughts—they become words.
Watch your words—they become actions.
Watch your actions—they become habits.
Watch your habits—they become character.
Watch your character—it becomes your destiny. [48]
—a leadership maxim

Dripping water bores a hole in the rock.
—Chinese proverb

When we teach our students Kung Fu, we have them repeat the same technique hundreds of time. In Kung Fu, we have a saying, "You have to repeat a technique a hundred times to learn it. You have to repeat it a thousand times to master it." Our goal is mastery of our techniques. As students are repeating their techniques, they say three phrases over and over:

"Repetition is the mother of skill."
"The more you do it, the better you get."
"The better you get, the more confidence you have."

Why do we practice? We practice to improve. We practice to master something. Take football for example, football practice is not held just to have a great practice. The purpose of practice is to condition the players to capture the wins necessary to arrive at the stadium for the ultimate showdown of blood, sweat, and tears. If you practice enough, you win. If you win enough at the game of football, you arrive at one of the most prestigious of all sporting events—the Super Bowl.

When we practice, we are training our muscles to respond the way they should in a game. Therefore, in practice we should train with the same intensity that we would use in a game. Someone once said, "Practice makes perfect." Another coach came along and amended that to say, "Perfect practice makes perfect." In Kung Fu Conditioning we teach our students, "How you train is how you will respond." In the martial arts, we are teaching self-defense tactics that are brutally effective. But if you practice them at half-speed, then you are teaching your muscles to respond at half-speed. That will not serve you if you ever find yourself in a position where you need to apply the self-defense tactics on the street. In our classes, we teach our students to play FULL OUT. How you practice is how you will play on the field. Therefore, you need to give your full heart to every practice session.

10. Confidence

For the true master, karate, kung-fu, aikido, wing-chun, and all the other martial arts are essentially avenues through which they can achieve spiritual serenity, mental tranquility, and the deepest self-confidence.[49]
—Joe Hyams, author and martial artist

Adopt a stance with the head erect, neither hanging down, nor looking up, not twisted. Your forehead and the space between your eyes should not be wrinkled. Do not roll your eyes nor allow them to blink, but slightly narrow them. With your features composed, keep the line of your nose straight with a feeling of slightly flaring your nostrils.[50]
—Miyamoto Musashi, samurai

Yes, I Can!

Confidence is the ability to believe in self. Whatever you believe in will happen. But it is more than the ability to believe in self. It is a belief that is based on your experience, your knowledge, and your abilities. Several things must happen for you to gain confidence:

> You must be willing to learn.
> You must be willing to practice.
> You must be willing to use what you learned.
> You must be willing to teach what you have learned and to share
> it with others.

In what areas are you most confident today? What areas would you like to improve the most? Do not allow FEAR (false evidence appearing real) to destroy your confidence. You must not retain the spirit of fear. Be defiant and believe you can move mountains. Build your confidence daily. Imitate what you would like to be and fake it until you make it. Speak aloud those things which are not yet in existence as though they exist now.

The actions in your life reflect your innermost feelings. Holding on to your past will restrict your future. Do not allow anyone to label you. Labels are remnants from your past experiences. Forgive yourself and liberate your feelings of guilt. You are worthy of success and you deserve it. You need a change of heart. This change of heart will produce your change of mind. Move into a new position and surround yourself with positive reinforcements. Find people who are willing to help you enhance your confidence and encourage you to step out of your comfort zone.

> **What is confidence? We can list some things that confidence is not.**
>
> Confidence is not pride.
> Confidence is not arrogance.
> Confidence is not aggression.
> Confidence is not rudeness.
> Confidence is not big talk or boasting.

A confident person doesn't have to boast. He lets his actions speak for him. What is the source of our confidence? Confidence comes from within. It comes from the heart. A quote from *The Martial Artist's Book of Five Rings* states, "The truth is that strength lies in the interior of the warrior: in his heart, his mind, and his spirit."[51]

Confidence and belief are very closely related. Do you believe in yourself? When others don't believe in you, do you still believe in yourself? When others put you down, do you give in to their negativity, or do you stand tall and believe in yourself? To be confident, we need to believe in ourselves.

Why do we need to believe in ourselves? Because if we don't believe in ourselves, then we carry disbelief and negativity wherever we go. Remember: You take you with you wherever you go. There is one person that you can never get away from—that person is you. So go ahead and believe in yourself. Have confidence. Think good thoughts about yourself.

As We Think In Our Hearts, So Are We

How you think about yourself is extremely important. The Bible teaches, "As we think in our hearts, so are we."[52] What do you think about yourself? The thoughts that are deep in your heart are the thoughts that are going to guide your life. Jou Tsung Hwa, a Tai Chi master, has written, "There is certainly some truth in the old adage, 'You are what you eat.' But how much more true that you are what you think." [53] If you think of yourself as a loser, then guess what, you will be a loser. If you think of yourself as a winner, then most of the time you will be a winner.

How do you think about yourself? Do you think of yourself as a winner? Envision yourself as a winner. See yourself wearing a black sash around your waist. See yourself scoring the game-winning touchdown. See yourself hoisting the winner's trophy above your head with thousands of cameras going off to capture this picture for the ages. These positive thoughts will help make you a winner.

Go look in a mirror. Now ask yourself, "Do you like what you see?" You are responsible for you. The only person that you can directly change is *you*. You can't change your parents. You can't change your brother or sister. But you can change you. Change takes effort. If you are not happy with the way you are, then it is worth the effort to change.

Confidence Comes From Experience

"It is not a shame to be knocked down by other people. The important thing is to ask when you're being knocked down, 'Why am I being knocked down?' If a person can reflect in this way, then there is hope for this person."[54]
—Bruce Lee, martial artist

Confident people are willing to try in spite of the fact that they might not succeed. Are you a risk taker? Confident people take risks. You must have heard, "Nothing ventured, nothing gained." The martial arts are about trying new things and taking risks. Drop deeper into your stances. Make each punch more deliberate than the last. Block each punch like you were destroying the opponent. Focus on each detail. Take risks.

Elite athletes take risks. Every time they suit up, every time they step on the court, the second the game clock begins; they are taking a risk. It takes confidence to step onto the field and play.

We gain confidence through experience. Take the example of a baby learning to walk. The baby tries and fails, tries and fails, tries and fails. But all the failures don't keep the little child from trying again and again. Through trying and failing, the baby learns how to walk. After the baby learns to walk, the baby learns to run. Just because you fail, you don't stop trying. You learn from your mistakes. You learn from experience. Get experience and gain confidence.

When it comes to the martial arts, we are all expected to try. The first time you try a drop stance, you might drop right on your behind. That's okay. Get up and try again. Your instructors aren't looking for perfection; they are looking for effort. Have the courage not to be perfect. After a few tries, you'll get it. After you get it, then you perfect it. Drop lower. Hold the stance longer. Make it the best drop stance that you can do.

Miyamoto Musashi in the classic *The Martial Artist's Book of Five Rings* says, "All men are the same except for their belief in their own selves, regardless of what others may think of them."[55] Decide not to let other people determine how you think about yourself. If they say you are a loser, then don't believe them. If they say that you will never amount to much, then disregard it. Only you can tell yourself what you are going to be.

Confidence and the Shaolin Athlete

I'm sure that we all want to be more confident people. But how can we become more confident? How can we walk like warriors?

Learn to Believe in Yourself

Belief is powerful. The idea of belief is the most powerful thing you can work on. Do you realize how powerful belief can be? Belief can change your perceptions of who you are as a person. When someone else believes in you (whether that someone is your coach, your mentor, your spouse, or your child), you begin to buy in to his or her belief. When they say, "You can do this," it brings courage to your heart. We need to hear our own voices say, "You can do this!" The power of belief can change your life.

But sometimes belief in self can be the most difficult thing in life. Why? Because we've been programmed not to believe in ourselves. We bought in to all the lies that other people have told us. "You can't do that." "You'll never succeed." "You'll never be a champion." "You're a loser." Lies, lies, lies.

We have to toss away the lies. We have to believe. Belief is powerful. Start believing in yourself today.

Four Ways to Build Your Confidence

1. Be willing to learn. Be a sponge and soak up everything that you can from any competent mentor or coach who is willing to teach you.

2. Be willing to practice. Remember, repetition is the mother of skill. The more you do it, the better you get. The better you get, the more confidence you have.

3. Use what you have learned.

4. Teach and share what you have learned with others. To really know something, you have to be able to teach it to others.

Learn To Think Positive Thoughts.

We need to keep positive thoughts in our mind. Thoughts are things. We need to treat thoughts like things, throw away the negative ones and keep the positive. Each day we should fill our mind with positive thoughts. At Edgewater Kung Fu, each student is expected to say, "Yes, I can!" each time they enter on or exit from the training mat. This "Yes, I Can!" attitude is an important part of our Kung Fu Conditioning program. Keeping this positive thought in your mind will help you become a more confident person.

Thinking positive thoughts is a good first step, but then we need to say those thoughts out loud so that we can hear them. When you say positive thoughts out loud and vocalize them, then they become more than just thoughts—they become affirmations. To affirm means to declare something to be true. When you vocalize a statement by saying it out loud, you say it and you hear it. That underscores the statement.

Affirmations are powerful. They can change the way you think and feel. This is why we say, "Yes I Can!" when we enter and exit the training floor. We want to always cling to powerful, positive affirmations. They can shape the way we see ourselves. They can make us confident leaders. Say to yourself, "I'm healthy; I'm wealthy; I'm fit; I've got a fighting spirit that will never quit." Now say it louder and with more passion. Now say, "I am so fortunate; I am so blessed; I am so lucky." Say this until you mean it. The positive thoughts will begin to penetrate into all areas of your life. Soon you will become what you have affirmed that you are.

11. Self-Image.

"Self-esteem and self-contempt have specific odors; they can be smelled."
—Eric Hoffer, American philosopher

What is self-image? Self-image is a reflection of who you think you are. Achievement begins here. It is a critical component of human personality and behavior. Outward change comes from within; it requires twenty-one days of conscious effort to have an effect. Many people feel they are inferior and do not see themselves as they really are. They do not believe they can enhance their self-image. Ask yourself, "Have I reached my optimum level of potential?" More than likely your answer is a definitive, "No." Each day we must continue to mature and develop in every aspect of our lives—our mind, our body, our emotions, and our spirit. Now is the time for a better self-image. This will increase your productivity, squash your fears, and be a catalyst for change.

Do not dwell on past failures. Do not compare yourself with others. Control your innermost thoughts. You and you alone are in control of your life. Look at yourself in a mirror. Do you like what you see? If not, then decide today that you will change. There is only one person in this world that you can never escape. Yourself! That's right— YOU take YOU with YOU wherever YOU go. Therefore, decide to change yourself. Decide to change your self-image. Learn to like yourself. Expect greatness. If you expect greatness, you will produce greatness. Discover the champion within. Begin today.

Ninety percent of everything you do is mental. If you want to succeed at anything, then you have to work twice as hard on yourself. You can have two people with great ability, but one will succeed and one will fail. Why? Because of the way they think. Because of their attitude. Not much separates professional athletes. Often it is how they think of themselves that makes the difference. Muhammad Ali's taunts of, "I am the greatest of all time!" weren't for show. He really believed that he was the greatest boxer in the history of the world. Michael Jordan knew that he was a champion. He wanted the ball in his hand when the game was close, because he had more confidence in himself than in any player on the court.

Kung Fu Conditioning teaches mental toughness. Mental toughness builds self-esteem. The more you overcome the little things in life (one extra pushup, one extra crunch, one additional minute in a horse stance), the more you believe that you can overcome anything in life. You start with small victories and then move on to bigger victories.

Kung Fu Conditioning doesn't just work on mental toughness (it will do that), but through the training, you also learn emotional toughness. The conditioning anchors you to an emotion. When you say, "I'm getting better and better every day in every way," you buy in to the idea that you are improving yourself. Your self-esteem rises. Or, when you say, "I can always do better than I think I can," you begin to live out that principle in your life. Denis Waitley, an American motivational speaker, writes, "Relentless, repetitive self talk is what changes our self-image."[56] We talk to ourselves every single day. What are you saying to yourself? The tapes that we play and replay in our heads determine our self-image. Think of yourself as a winner. Notify yourself that you are great. In doing this, you build your self-image.

12. Inspiration.

You often hear about motivation in athletics. Instead of talking about motivation, let's talk about inspiration. Look at the word *INSPIRATION* for a moment. What do you see? You see the words *SPIRIT* and *IN*. Inspiration means that we have the right *SPIRIT IN* us. Inspiration last longer than motivation. Motivation isn't permanent. Motivation comes and goes. But when you have the right spirit, you take that spirit with you wherever you go. Whether you are on the field or on the court or in the training gym or at home or in the mall. When you are an inspired person, you have the right spirit inside of you.

As you progress as an athlete, you get inspired. Inspiration isn't something you are taught. Inspiration is caught. Inspiration is experienced. You must remember your ultimate goal—to do your personal best every single day. There is always someone waiting on the sideline to take your place. They are there, just waiting for you not to be at your peak.

You have to envision yourself as a winner. You have to let go of any negative images that you have. Remember how far you have come. Remember why you are doing this. What is your ultimate goal? This is your choice. You have chosen to be an athlete. It is a great choice. You have the opportunity to go to work and do what you love to do. Also, you get to be great at doing it. A very small percentage of people in the world have what it takes to excel in a sport. You have what it takes. That should inspire you to always do your personal best. Have a great appreciation for who you are and what you do.

As athletes, every day that you play, you have to do your best. If you are on a team, you are playing not just for yourself, but for the team. Allow your teammates to inspire you. If you play an individual sport like golf or tennis, you still have people who are pulling for you to do your best. Never give less than your best effort.

To accomplish great success in athletics takes inspiration. What inspires you? How do you get ready for a game? This is an age of psychological coaches and sports gurus. That's okay. It's good to have someone who can help you visualize greatness. We've already discussed the need for mentors and coaches. But at some point, you have to play the game yourself. Your coach or mentor can't play for you. When you are in the game, you have to be able to motivate yourself. Ask yourself— who motivates the motivator? The motivator does. And YOU are the motivator.

Keys to Being an Inspired Shaolin Athlete

- Learn what motivates you (winning, success, fear, pain, goals, greatness).
- Motivation has ups and downs. Never position yourself to stay down.
- Remember: Positive brings forth positive; excitement brings forth excitement; belief brings forth belief; inspiration brings forth more inspiration.
- Inspiration creates a strong burning desire that will lead to a positive mental attitude.

---

13. Meditation

Martial meditation is a training to resist evil in the world. Religious meditation is frequently conceived as a kind of training for the rigors of the moral life.[57]
—Michael Raposa, Professor of Religious Studies at Lehigh University

Now and again, it is necessary to seclude yourself among deep mountains and hidden valleys to restore your link to the source of life. Sit comfortably and first contemplate the manifest realm of existence. This realm is concerned with externals, the physical form of things. Then fill your body with ki and sense the manner in which the universe functions—its shape, its color, and its vibrations. Breathe in and let yourself soar to the ends of the universe; breathe out and bring the cosmos back inside. Next, breathe up all the fecundity and vibrancy of the earth. Finally, blend the breath of heaven and the breath of earth with that of your own body, becoming the breath of life itself. As you calm down, naturally let yourself settle in the heart of things. Find your center, and fill yourself with light and heat. [58]

—Morihei Ueshiba

Before our STORM team workouts at Edgewater Kung Fu, we always begin with a few minutes of standing meditation. Why? Because meditation helps focus the mind and it prepares us to train. In meditation we try to empty ourselves of anything that would distract us from our training. We also try to place ourselves in the moment in order to have the best training session possible. This places us in a state of peak mental and physical performance.

Meditation is very important in the martial arts. Some forms of Kung Fu practice "moving meditation." Michael L. Raposa in his book *Meditation and the Martial Arts* writes:

Without denying their identity as fighting arts, it is important to observe that Taijiquan and Baguazhang are perceived as spiritual exercises to a greater extent than most other classical or contemporary martial disciplines. Indeed, the Taiji individual form is very likely the one activity most frequently characterized by both scholars and practitioners as a type of "moving meditation." Bagua circle-walking, although less well-known and not as widely performed, especially outside of China, may be even more aptly described in this fashion. [59]

Whether you practice "moving meditation" or "standing meditation," meditation is an important ingredient in martial arts training.

Meditation gives us focus. The focus that is gained from meditation should continue throughout each training session. We should apply that focus to everything we do. Herman Kauz in *A Path to Liberation* writes:

At first glance, martial arts practice does not appear to be meditation. Kata, or form practice, may look like a dance, and practice with a partner may look like a competition or a violent encounter. What seems to make an activity meditative is the way we use the mind in its pursuit. Thus, where a martial art is taught as a meditative discipline, students are urged to invest their thought fully in what they are doing. An extraneous thought may intrude but is ignored in favor of continued concentration on the unfolding action."[60]

So throughout our training, we have to stay focused and meditate on the task at hand. Practicing meditation helps develop focus. When you start to get distracted, think of something that you can do or say that will help you get back to focus. Football players often slap their helmets. One tennis player wears a rubber band on one wrist and pops it before every serve. You might say something to yourself. Your word might be "warrior." Or your phrase might be "Back to focus." It might be "Yes, I can!" Find a word or a phrase that brings you back to focus.

Meditation not only helps with focus, it also helps us deal with stress in our lives. Chi Gong exercises like the ones taught in this Kung Fu Conditioning program have been proven stress-busters. Stress is a part of life. Our ability or inability to handle stress has a great impact on our general health. Too much stress causes our endocrine system to pump out stress hormones to the point that our bodies become out of balance biochemically and our cells degenerate. Meditation can interrupt this process.

Simple Ways to Practice Meditation

1. Sit down, close your eyes, and focus on your breathing. Empty your mind by focusing on your breath.
2. Close your eyes and say a positive phrase over and over.

14. Self-Control.

What is self-control? To "control" means to have power over something. Self-control means to have power over self. Self-control is the ability to control one's behavior, one's actions, one's reactions, and one's impulses. To have self-control, one must have control of both the body and the mind. The best way to keep anything from controlling you is to have control over yourself.

Michael L. Raposa writes, "The essence of control is self-control: One can prevail against an external foe only if one has first achieved internal self-mastery. From another perspective, external conflicts between persons arise only because conflicts within persons already exist and remain unsolved."[61] If we are going to control any area of our lives—our language, our temper, our sexual desires, our laziness—then we need to have self-control. This means we must practice internal self-mastery.

The Apostle Paul uses the analogy of an athlete in training to describe how we must train our spirit. Paul also taught an important lesson about self-control. He wrote, "Everyone who competes in the games goes into strict training. They do it to get a crown that will not last; but we do it to get a crown that will last forever. Therefore I do not run like a man running aimlessly; I do not fight like a man beating the air. No, I beat my body and make it my slave so that after I have preached to others, I myself will not be disqualified for the prize" (1 Corinthians 9:25–27). Paul said, "I beat my body and make it my slave."[62] Why did he do this? He did it for self-control. In the martial arts, we beat our bodies and our bodies take a beating. When we train our bodies in this way, we are learning self-control.

What Is the Difference Between Self-control and Self-discipline?

When we looked at the subject of focus, we asked about the difference between focus and concentration. We saw that concentration is the thought process, and focus is the application of concentration. So focus is a part of concentration. In the same way, self-control is a part of a larger concept called self-discipline. Using the analogy of art, self-discipline is the overall composition and design, and self-control is the detail work in the individual brushstrokes.

Self-discipline is about the attitude. In self-discipline we force our behavior to be a certain way until that behavior becomes automatic. We can apply this definition to all areas of our lives including school, religion, family, friendships, sports, and the martial arts. Do we have an attitude of self-discipline when it comes to our chores, our schoolwork, and our martial arts training?

Self-control is about controlling our emotions. It is about internal control. Self-control means that we control our temperament. Self-control determines how we will react in specific situations. When someone is angry with us, do we return anger with anger? When we feel frustrated, do we give up or do we persevere? How do we handle conflict? How do we handle stress? These are all areas where we need self-control.

Without any control, there is chaos. Without self-control there is chaos in life. The Shaolin Athlete needs to be an example of control. By demonstrating control, the athlete will expel chaos from his or her life.

There is a time and a place for everything. There is a time to be humble and a time to be confident. There is even a time and a place to act crazy. There is a time to demonstrate emotion. The athlete must know when to apply these different attributes and emotions. Self-control allows us to harness our emotions and allow them to drive our actions in the right way.

In life, our egos take a beating. Someone calls us a name. Another person belittles us. Someone else ignores us. Another person spreads rumors about us. Another person pushes our buttons just to be an irritant. What do we do in these situations? Do we retaliate? Do we resort to physical violence?

Sifu Romain teaches, "If you find yourself in a fight, then you've already made your first mistake." Self-control will keep us out of fights. Self-control will allow us to walk or to run away from potentially violent situations.

Two Ways That the Martial Arts Teach Self-Control

1. Stance Training.

An essential ingredient in the strength, power, and effectiveness of a martial artist is his or her stances. The stance is our root. Morihei Ueshiba wrote, "Every sturdy tree that towers over human beings owes its existence to a deeply rooted core."[63] If a tree doesn't have a strong root, then it will be blown over by the wind. If the martial artist doesn't have a strong root, then he or she will be toppled by an opponent. Therefore, stance training is an important part of martial arts training.

For hundreds of years at the Shaolin Temple in China, before a student was accepted into training, he had to demonstrate the strength of his horse stance (his *Ma Bu*). He would stand outside the temple day after day, perfecting his horse stance. This took self-control. He had to fight through the pain. There were moments when he wanted to quit, to go back to his home village. But he pushed through the pain because of his desire to be trained by the masters. This type of training teaches self-control.

2. Taking Instruction From an Instructor

To learn, you have to be teachable. It takes humility. You have to walk into class like a beginner. Self-control gives you the humility to become successful in the martial arts. After 10 years, you still need training. After 30 years, you still need to seek out training. When you find that training, then you need to bring to it the attitude of a beginner. You need to stand on your dot like it was the first time you ever stepped on a training mat and be a learner. This takes self-control.

Even if you know more that the person who is teaching the class, you stay humble and learn. When you train, you take on the heart of student. And the student is not above the teacher. This teaches us humility. And humility teaches us self-control.

Without self-control, we will not be teachable. Every time we take a class, we need to have the attitude of a beginner and act as if we were training for the first time.

15. Be a Success.

To laugh often and much;
To win the respect of intelligent people and the affection of children;
To earn the appreciation of honest critics and endure the betrayal of false friends;
To appreciate beauty;
To find the best in others;
To leave the world a bit better, whether by a healthy child, a garden patch, or a redeemed social condition;
To know even one life has breathed easier because you have lived.
This is to have succeeded.

—Ralph Waldo Emerson

Don't settle for anything less than being the very best athlete that you can be. What will it take for you to be successful as a Shaolin Athlete? Your goal should be constant and never-ending improvement. Consider this: How tall does a tree grow? The answer is: As tall as it possibly can grow. The *Shaolin Athlete* must always reach for the sky in an effort to constantly and continually improve. Success is a choice. Here are some steps that can help you travel down the road of success.

First, you must believe in yourself. Someone once said, "The only limitation is limitation."[64] Don't limit yourself. Don't settle for less than the best that you can be. You must decide what you are going to believe and what you are not going to believe. You control your beliefs. Believe that you will succeed.

You might have heard the story of the two shoe salesmen who went to sell shoes in an obscure village in Africa. When they arrived, they saw that none of the villagers wore shoes. The first salesman called his headquarters and said, "I'm sorry, but our company is not going to sell any shoes in this village because none of the villagers wear shoes." The other salesperson phoned his home office with a very different message, "Quick!" he said, "Send an extra shipment of shoes! None of these villagers wear shoes! This is the perfect place to sell shoes!" What was the difference between the successful shoe salesman and the unsuccessful one? Belief.

Second, keep yourself in a peak mental state. Athletes have to do their very best every single day. You can't wait until game time to give your best. A winning attitude isn't just saved for the field of play. A winning attitude needs to go with the Shaolin Athlete at all times.

If you find yourself slipping from your peak mental state, find a way to remind yourself to snap back into focus. In Kung Fu class, we clap our hands and say, "Back to focus." You might not want to do this at a corporate board meeting, but find some ritual that will help you get back to focus. You might snap your fingers and whisper to yourself, "Back to focus." You might slap yourself on the leg and say, "Here we go. Give it your all." Some athletes slap themselves in the face as a reminder to stay focused. Find something that works for you. Find an action and a phrase that will remind you to get back to your peak mental state. This will help you be the best athlete and the best person that you can be.

Third, be a person of action. Massive action gets massive results. Don't sit around waiting for a golden opportunity to drop in your lap. You have to make your opportunities. After you make your opportunities, then you have to make the most out of every opportunity.

Never underestimate what you can accomplish in a single day. You can do more than you imagine. But you have to get started. Once you start, the battle is already half over. Get up and get going.

Twelve Principles Of Success

1. Love the process.

Success is a process and not a destination. People say, "When I accomplish x, y, and z, then I'll truly be happy." But this isn't true. You have to fall in love with the process. If you succeed in the loving the process, then you'll succeed in life.

2. Be a giver.

When you give, you receive. Everywhere you go, give a blessing.

3. Be teachable.

In the martial arts, you are always a student. Come to class with your cup empty.

4. Be persistent.

"I will persist until I succeed." Dripping water can bore a hole through a rock.

5. Learn to let go.

Let go of anything that will keep you from your goals. When you make a mistake, learn from it; and try again. "You never fail until you stop trying."

6. Be a leader.

Leaders are not remembered for what they took, but for what they gave. Leaders influence others.

7. Demonstrate self-discipline.

Do what needs to be done, when it needs to be done, whether you want to do it or not.

8. Visualize.

See what you want to become. Picture it clearly in your mind. If you can picture it in your mind, then you can accomplish it in your life.

9. Believe.

Belief can move mountains. In order to succeed, you have to believe.

10. Create.

Once you visualize where you want to go, don't linger. Go! Go realize your dreams.

11. Be a model.

Be a model, instead of a critic. Don't judge others. Be a light for others to follow. Mohandas Gandhi said, "You must be the change you want to see in the world."

12. Work on you.

The only person whom you can change is you.

16. The Gift of Choice: Making Wise Choices.

It is our choices…that show us what we truly are, far more than our abilities.
—J. K. Rowling, from *Harry Potter and the Chamber of Secrets*

The future is not a result of choices among alternative paths offered by the present, but a place that is created—created first in the mind and will, created next in activity. The future is not some place we are going to, but one we are creating. The paths are not to be found, but made, and the activity of making them, changes both the maker and the destination. [65]

—John Schaar, futurist

Have you ever seen the Indiana Jones movies? These movies are great action adventure movies. The first one is a classic, *Indiana Jones and the Raiders of the Lost Ark*. This seems like a perfect movie (and there are far too few perfect movies in the world). In the third movie, *Indiana Jones and the Last Crusade*, Indiana Jones is searching for the Holy Grail, the cup used by Jesus in the Last Supper. After enduring many tests to find the cup, Indiana discovers a room that is filled with many cups that could have been the one used by Jesus at the Last Supper. Some of the cups have jewels embedded in them. Some of them are polished gold. Indiana is told by an ancient Knight Templar to choose wisely. Indiana chose a cup that had no jewels, wasn't polished, in fact, was quite ordinary. He chose it because it looked like the cup of a carpenter. He made a wise choice.

Choose Wisely

Life is all about choices. We not only need to make wise choices, but we need to be zealous in our choices. We need to put our heart into the choices that we make.

We aren't perfect. And attempting to be a perfectionist is tiring and futile.

I heard the story of man who was a perfectionist and whenever it would snow, he would pay close attention to radio announcements because he wanted to make sure he parked his car in the proper spot. One morning he heard the radio announcer say, "Today we will have 6 to 8 inches of snow so park your car on the even-numbered side of the street so that the snow plow can get through." Another day he heard, "Today we will have 8 to 10 inches of snow so park your car on the odd-numbered side of the street so that the snow plow can get through." On another occasion the announcer said, "Today we will have 10 to 12 inches of snow." The man was distraught. He looked at his wife and asked her, "The announcer didn't say which side of the street I should park on. What am I going to do?" The wife, with the loving patience of a woman who has live for years with a perfectionist, said, "Honey, why don't you just leave the car in the garage this time?"

No one is perfect. But we can train ourselves to make wise choices. As athletes, we need to learn how to feed our bodies. We need to listen to our bodies when they are fatigued. We need to stay hydrated before a game. We need to learn how to manage our lives. We need to learn to choose wisely.

We believe that everyone can live a great life. We believe that you can consistently grow and mature. You don't have to wallow in a quagmire of mediocrity, ineffectiveness, and unproductiveness. You can have more than good days; you can have great days. And if you add together enough great days, then you have a great year. It has been said, "If you take care of the days, then the years will take care of themselves." Great days lead to great weeks, which lead to great months, which lead to great years.

Have you ever seen an eagle or a hawk soar in the sky? It is a beautiful, majestic sight. Speaking metaphorically, you can soar like an eagle. All you have to do is make wise choices every day.

You have to believe that your choices make a difference. They make a difference in your own life. They make a difference in the life of your family. They make a difference in your world. Dwight D. Eisenhower said, "The history of free man is never written by chance but by choice—their choice." What kind of choices are you making?

There are some things you can't choose. You can't choose your past. It is already behind you. You can't choose your parents. They made that choice for you. You can't choose the environment where you were raised. Someone else made that choice for you. You can't choose your genetic makeup. That's already been written in your DNA. You can't choose your genes, but you can chose how you will respond to them. You can choose your present and your future. You can create the world in which you live. You can reinvent yourself every single day. You can shape your future. This creating, reinventing, and shaping comes by means of our choices.

We live in a culture of victimization and a culture of blame. What do we mean by that? We live in an environment where it is easy for people to deflect the blame for their mistakes from themselves to someone else. We blame our parents, our upbringing, our ignorance, our emotional makeup, or our genetic makeup. It is easy to shift the blame and pull out the victim card. Athletes get caught using steroids, and they blame it on the guy in the locker next to them. Politicians get caught in a lie, and they blame it on some junior staffer in their organization.

We need to realize that between the stimulus and the response there is that precious moment of choice.

Stimulus] [Choice] [Response

Stephen Covey writes about this concept. He states, "Between stimulus and response there is a space. In that space lies our freedom and power to choose our response. In those choices lie our growth and happiness."[66] Our growth and our happiness lie in our choices.

1. Reinvent yourself every day. Choose how you will live each day.

We choose how we are going to live out each day, and what we are going to do with the day. Every single day, the sun rises and begins a new day for all of us. With the rising of the sun, you decide how the day will go. Do you cling to the bitterness and disappointments of the day that has just passed? Do you wallow in the mire of self-pity that covered you during the past twenty-four hours? Do you settle for another day of mediocrity? It is your choice. Your get to reinvent yourself every day. Every day you are a new creation.

Therefore, this day, say, I choose to:

> Be the best husband or wife that I can possibly be.
> Be the best father or mother that I can possibly be.
> Be the best daughter or son that I can possibly be.
> Be the best student that I can possibly be.
> Be the best friend that I can possibly be.
> Be the best employer or employee that I can possibly be.
> Be the best athlete that I can be.
> Be the best martial artist that I can be.
> Be the best person that I can possibly be.

This doesn't mean that you won't stumble. This doesn't mean that you won't make mistakes. This doesn't mean that you won't make wrong decisions. But when you make wrong choices, then you stop, think, and reinvent yourself in that moment. You recalibrate where you are in that moment and recommit to being your best for the rest of the day. Remember the saying, "If you take care of the days, the years will take care of themselves." This saying is true of minutes and hours as well. To have a great day, you have to be at your best during the minutes and hours of the day.

2. Periodically take time for self-examination.

We go to the doctor for physicals. We go to the dentist for checkups. We change the oil in our cars every so often and get a mechanic to look over them. Take time for self-inventory.

Write down what is important to you. Write down your priorities in life. As a father or mother, what is important to you? What are your goals as an athlete? What are your goals as a martial artist? What do you want to accomplish in your life? What will your legacy be?

Now set other goals—yearly goals, weekly goals, daily goals—that reflect this vision for your life. Now go make choices that reflect this vision and these goals.

A simple exercise that everyone can do to help with productivity is this—just before you go to bed every night, write down three things that you want to accomplish the next day. Make sure these three daily goals fit into your legacy goal. Then the first thing in the morning, look at these goals and meditate over them. Then go and accomplish them that day.

But take time to examine your life and to examine the vision you have for your life. Stephen Covey gives four assumptions that are worth exploring:

1. For the *body*—assume you've had a heart attack; now live accordingly.
2. For the *mind*—assume the half-life of your profession is two years; now prepare accordingly.
3. For the *heart*—assume everything you say about another, they can overhear; now speak accordingly.
4. For the *spirit*—assume you have a one-on-one visit with your Creator every quarter; now live accordingly.[67]

Life is all about choices. It is about making wise choices. The most important moments that we live in life are those moments, that little space, between stimulus and response. To make the right choice in the moment, we have to set our minds to be the best that we can be. Set your mind. Decide.

17. R.E.S.T.

A simple acronym can help you remember four key points to become a more successful person. The acronym is R.E.S.T. and the four points are: Read, Exercise, Sleep, and Think. Let's break these down:

Read. Readers are leaders. Read to succeed. Reading helps us develop communication skills and reasoning power. To be a success you have to be able to communicate clearly and effectively with people. Reading strengthens your vocabulary. Reading fuels your mind. If you aren't a reader, then become one. Reading will help you achieve your dreams and will help you climb the ladder of success.

Exercise. To have a healthy mind, you need a healthy body. Exercise rejuvenates the body. Exercise makes you feel better, and when you feel better, you are more productive. Proper nutrition and proper exercise are essential for a healthy, balanced, successful life.

Sleep. To be your best throughout the day, the body needs sleep. Different people require different amounts of sleep. Doctors suggest that you get somewhere between seven to nine hours of sleep every night. Teenagers need more sleep than young adults. Find what works best for you. Once you discover how much sleep you need to function at your highest level, then commit to getting that amount of sleep every night.

Think. Successful people are thinkers. When handed a problem, they are able to reason through the problem until they find a solution. The IBM corporation used this single word as their corporate motto: THINK. How much time out of the day do you spend thinking about what you want to accomplish and how you are going to accomplish it? Time spent in concentrated thought is time well spent.

18. Live in the Moment

Life is within death, death is within life; you must exist right here, right now.
—Morihei Ueshiba

In the movie, *The Dead Poets Society*, Robin Williams plays an English teacher who takes a job at a boys' prep school in New England in 1959. He teaches spoiled, rich kids the English classics. The teacher uses unusual methods to reach the boys. He has them rip pages out of their English text that he deems unworthy of study. He introduces modern, popular songs to the class. Once he has their attention, he then begins to teach them about the great, lasting themes of English literature. One such theme is a phrase that he uses over and over again with his students—*Carpe diem. Carpe diem* means, "Seize the day."

Seize the day! Get the most out of every day that you are given. All you are guaranteed in life is the present moment. The past is gone, the future is uncertain, the present stares you in the face like a tiger ready to pounce. What will you do with the present moment?

When you live each moment to its fullest, you end up having full, gratifying days. Gratifying days make a successful week. Successful weeks turn into a prosperous month. And prosperous months result in a fulfilling and bountiful year. But it all starts with a single moment.

When you waste a moment, it's gone. You can never recover that moment again. Waste enough moments and your life will pass you by like a fleeting ship sailing through the night. That is is one reason why each moment is precious.
Henry David Thoreau wrote, "I went into the woods because I wanted to live deliberately. I wanted to live deep and suck out all the marrow of life...to put to rout all that was not life; and not, when I came to die, discover that I had not lived." Live life deliberately. Suck the marrow out of life. Drink of life like it is a superb wine. Live each moment to the fullest. *Carpe diem!*

You don't know what tomorrow will bring. Therefore, live today to its fullest. Believe and act.

Ask yourself: If not now, when?

19. *Kaizen*

Kaizen is a Japanese word that means "constant and never ending improvement." As an athlete, you have to challenge yourself continually. You need to surround yourself with people who will challenge you, but ultimately, YOU have to be your hardest coach. You have to be more intense than anyone else.

The Paradoxical Commandments
by Kent M. Keith

People are illogical, unreasonable and self-centered. Love them anyway.

If you do good, people will accuse you of selfish ulterior motives. Do good anyway.

If you are successful, you will win false friends and true enemies. Succeed anyway.

The good you do today will be forgotten tomorrow. Do good anyway.

Honesty and frankness make you vulnerable. Be honest and frank anyway.

The biggest men and women with the biggest ideas can be shot down by the smallest men and women with the smallest minds. Think big anyway.

People favor underdogs but follow only top dogs. Fight for a few underdogs anyway.

What you spend years building may be destroyed overnight. Build anyway.

People really need help but may attack you if you do help them. Help people anyway.

Give the world the best you have and you'll get kicked in the teeth. Give the world the best you have anyway.[68]

20. Leadership

With good leaders
When their work is done
Their task fulfilled
The people will say:
"We have done it ourselves."

—Tao Te Ching, no. 60

Shaolin Athletes are leaders. They are leaders on the field and in life. But they don't lead with force. They learn that the use of force causes counterforce. Shaolin Athletes learn to lead by influence and example.

Great leaders are not born; they are made or developed. They are remembered by what they gave and not by what they took. Their leadership came over a period of time. It was a process.

Kung Fu Conditioning is leadership training. How? When you persevere through your training exercises, you are conditioning not just your body but your mind and spirit as well. You will be challenged. Whatever your issues are, they will come up in class. If you have a problem with authority, it will be revealed. If you have an anger problem, it will surface. Once these problems arise, then we can work together on these problems to change your character.

Think of a diamond. When someone digs a diamond out of the ground or sifts it from the water, it is just a stone. After a master craftsman cuts and polishes the stone, then it sparkles. Its intrinsic traits have to be brought out of the stone by a trained expert. That is what Kung Fu Conditioning will do for you. You will be challenged to grow. You will be challenged to be a leader.

Sinking into and holding a horse stance teaches you courage. Seeing yourself as a black sash teaches vision. Reaching your goals teaches self-discipline, and self-discipline is the master key to success. When you make mistakes, you learn to push through. You learn perseverance.

Lead by Influence

A platoon leader doesn't get his platoon to go by getting up and shouting and saying, 'I am smarter. I am bigger. I am stronger. I am the leader.' He gets men to go along with him because they want to do it for him and they believe in him.

—Dwight D. Eisenhower

Friendliness, kindness toward others will create a spirit unparalleled in loyalty. Followers will take upon themselves… hardship and sacrifice toward the attainment of goals….It is necessary that the leader have firmness and correctness within, and an encouraging attitude toward others.

—I Ching, no. 58

Leaders lead. But how do good leaders lead? Leaders lead through influence. Good leadership is not just a position or a title. Good leadership is not about authority and power. Good leadership is not about bullying people around. Good leadership is not about seeing who can get the most followers. Good leadership is learning how to influence people.

You lead by influencing people. You give people hope. You point people to victory. You spend time reflecting on each person on your team and you ask, "How can I get the best out of this person?" You stay positive. You don't control or manipulate people. You teach people how to self-govern their lives. This engenders respect.

Lead by Example

Be a pattern to others, and then all will go well.

—Cicero

Who would you rather follow? Would you rather follow someone who tells you what to do, or would you rather follow someone who models what you want to become?

Most of us can remember a coach who barked orders at us, cursed in our faces, and even some who were physically abusive. Thankfully, these types of coaches are no longer the norm. We no longer live in an age where we can say, "Do what I say, but don't do what I do." People will not tolerate that type of hypocrisy. People are looking at the whole of a person's life. They want to follow leaders who are genuine.

The Shaolin Athlete understands that for every action, there is a reaction. When we lead by control, manipulation, and disrespect, we breed anger, bitterness, and resentment. Negativity creates negativity. When you treat an athlete with respect, they will respond by giving their best. Encouragement draws the best out of a person. As a Shaolin Athlete, you treat other people the way you would like to be treated in every situation. You lead, not by force, but by example.

Dale Carnegie once said, "There is only one way under high Heaven to get anybody to do anything. Did you ever stop to think of that? Yes, just one way. And that is by making the other person want to do it. Remember, there is no other way."

Shaolin Athletes are leaders. We lead by influence, and we lead by example. Leadership is a decision, not a position. Decide and lead.

How to Be a More Charismatic Leader

Smile.

Say people's names. People love to hear their name.

To be interesting, be interested. Ask questions.

Speak "for" and not "against" things.

Give *sincere* compliments.

Accept compliments gracefully.

In order to be respected, give respect.

Say what you mean and mean what you say.

Stand straight and tall.

Think confident thoughts.

PART IV

THE SHAOLIN ATHLETE'S BODY

GOOD FOR THE BODY IS THE WORK OF THE BODY,
GOOD FOR THE SOUL THE WORK OF THE SOUL,
AND GOOD FOR EITHER THE WORK OF THE OTHER.

—HENRY DAVID THOREAU

Often, when you buy a product, it comes with care and maintenance instructions. When you buy a new car, it comes with an owner's manual that tells you how often you must change the oil and rotate the tires. When you buy a new iPad, it comes with information on the care and maintenance of the world's sleekest and coolest tablet. Unfortunately, the human body doesn't come with such instructions. When we arrive in the world, we don't come with an owner's manual. So we have to write our own owner's manual. We have to figure out for ourselves about the care and maintenance of our bodies.

Fortunately, there are places where we can turn for help in writing our owner's manual. The first place that we can turn is to our very own body. If we listen to our own body, then we will gather data that we can place in the manual. If we don't listen, then we will lose the data. To write the owner's manual to your own body, begin by listening to your body. When do you get overly tired? Where are the aches and pains? Which foods do you digest easily and which are difficult to digest? How often can you exercise without tearing down your body? Find the answers to these questions, and put them in the owner's manual.

A second place where we can go for help in writing the owner's manual for our bodies is to modern, scientific studies on the human body and exercise. Over the last decade, great research has been done on the human body and conditioning. Since sports represent big money, sports medicine is also big money. So scientists have been studying the best ways for athletes to take care of their bodies. But each body is different. And each body's reaction to playing a sport is different. Therefore, you have to take the results of the research in sports medicine and study it to make sure that it fits your own body.

A third place where we can go for help in writing our own owner's manual is to the vast body of literature from Chinese medicine. Kung Fu Conditioning exercises were originally invented to strengthen the bodies and minds of Buddhist priests. Taoist priests invented Chi Gong exercises to strengthen the body. Taoist priests studied internal alchemy as a means of discovering longevity and immortality. Therefore, these studies will greatly enrich the writing of your own personal owner's manual.

Here are some helpful hints as you write your own Owner's Manual for your body:

Aqua Please

Hydration is the key to energy. We are mostly water. When you get dehydrated, you feel fatigue, get a headache, and have low energy. When you stay hydrated, those problems go away. Also, water purifies the body. It cleanses your body of toxins.

Drink before, during and after the workout. Learn what works best for you. Everyone is different. So figure out what is best for you.

Feed Me!

What should I eat and how often should I eat? Books and books have been written about proper nourishment for athletes. There are many different theories about what is best. Should I eat a low carbohydrate and high protein diet or should I eat a low protein and high carbohydrate diet? Everyone's body is different. Therefore you have to develop a diet that suits your body type. You have to begin by listening to your own body.

- Natural, unprocessed, whole foods are healthier than processed foods.
- Stay away from fried foods and foods that are high in saturated fat.
- Eat plenty of fruits and vegetables.
- Drink water and avoid sugary drinks.

Don't Forget to Stretch

One of the most important aspects of athletic training is stretching. Stretching gives the athlete long, lean muscles that are able to endure rigorous training exercises and combat on the field of play. When you stretch, stretch to the point of discomfort without pain. Pain is the signal to ease back a bit. Stretch after you have warmed up the muscles. Stretch at the beginning and the end of exercising. Make stretching a part of your daily routine. And when you stretch, visualize your muscles elongating. Stretching helps avoid injury.

Keeping it Fun

"When the fun stops, pay attention; pain is probably not far behind." [69]
—James E. Loehr, sports trainer

Why did you get into sports in the first place? Most likely, you starting playing your sport because it was fun. Don't lose the joy of sports. Keep it fun. Mix up your training. Train with people you enjoy being around.

How often should I train?

Kung Fu Conditioning can be done every day, but it is always good to rest at least one day a week. Again, listen to your body. If you aren't sleeping well at night, that can be a sign of overtraining. Cut back and see if you sleep better. Kung Fu Conditioning is strenuous and will create soreness in your muscles. You will use muscles that aren't often used when training as a Shaolin Athlete. You can often train through the soreness. But you have to be able to delineate between soreness and injury. Pain is often the sign of an injury. Injuries need to heal so that more damage will not be done. Learn to tell the difference between pain and soreness, between soreness and injury. The rule of thumb is: Work through soreness and rest through pain. When in question consult a sports therapist or a medical doctor. Learn to listen to your body.

It is better to train twenty to thirty minutes a day, four or five times a week, than to attempt to exercise an hour or two once a week. Regularity and consistency is key. The length and consistency of your workouts depends on how much you want to get from your workout. But again, it is important to listen to your body and not over train.

PART V

GETTING STARTED:
WHERE DO YOU GO FROM HERE?

WITH THE WARRIOR MIND-SET, YOU'LL PATTERN YOUR LIFE AROUND THE PURSUIT OF EXCELLENCE. INDEED, THE MARTIAL WAY IS A DISCIPLINE DEVOTED TO THE PERFECTION OF CHARACTER. IT'S A VERY PERSONAL PURSUIT IN WHICH THE STUDENT TURNS HIS ATTENTION INWARD. HE EVALUATES THE STRENGTH OF HIS SPIRIT AND SETS ABOUT POLISHING THOSE FACETS THAT NEED WORK. SO INSTEAD OF BEING A CARPENTER OR A LAWYER WHO DOES A MARTIAL ART AS A HOBBY, YOU'LL BE A WARRIOR, PRACTICING BOTH YOUR CAREER AND YOUR ART TO HONE YOUR SPIRIT. WITH THAT APPROACH, YOU CAN'T HELP BUT ACHIEVE IN YOUR CHOSEN VOCATION, WHATEVER IT MAY BE.[70]

—FORREST E. MORGAN, MAJOR USAF

A Program to Follow.

The way of the Shaolin Athlete is a life-changing journey. It causes us to look deep within ourselves to see who we are and what we want to become. It is a lifelong journey. It is a difficult journey. Sifu Romain's desire is for you to continue and to complete what you have started. Now that you have begun this program—the Shaolin Athlete/Kung Fu Conditioning—decide that you will continue your journey following the way of the Shaolin Athlete.

We hope that you will continue to pursue your martial arts training from qualified academies and instructors where you live. But beware, not all academies and not all instructors are the same. In fact, the most important decision that the martial artist will ever make concerning training is in deciding who will be his or her instructor.

Nicklaus Suino, in his book *Arts of Strength, Arts of Serenity*, offers this advice:

> It is commonly said that you would not be wasting your time even if you spent a year or two looking for the right teacher. That may be an exaggeration, but you should definitely make sure that your teacher is well educated in his or her art, and that he or she offers a safe, positive learning environment. Go and watch a class at the school you are thinking of training at, and pay close attention to the attitude and teaching style of the head instructor (or subordinates or senior students if this instructor is not teaching at the time). [71]

This is great advice. Attend a class. Ask yourself, "Does this class feel right to me? Does this instructor feel right?" If not, move on to another school. If yes, then give your heart to Kung Fu Conditioning and become a Shaolin Athlete.

Sticking With It.

When running a race, it doesn't matter how quickly you begin, if you are unable to finish. The same is true in life. The important quality of any health and fitness program is consistency. In our Kung Fu Conditioning classes, students will often encourage each other by shouting, "Finish strong!" Once you start something, you are going to want to finish. The Shaolin Athlete finishes what he or she starts. "Finish strong!"

There is a Chinese saying that goes, *"Hu tou she wie."* This means, "Tiger head, snake tail." This describes starting something with all the energy and zeal of a tiger, but ending with the slithering of a snake's tail, as when we begin a project with great intensity, but then quit before the job is finished. Don't let this phrase apply to your endeavor to be a Shaolin Athlete. Start like a tiger and finish like a tiger. Finish strong!

In Kung Fu Conditioning, there is so much to learn and experience. You will always feel like a beginner. There are dozens of styles and moves to learn and explore. Once you have begun to experience the growth physically, emotionally, mentally, and spiritually that comes from Kung Fu Conditioning, decide that you are going to continue training and that you are going to take your training to a new level. Set goals for yourself. Set your goal to become a Black Sash. Continue to better yourself through Kung Fu Conditioning.

Remember that Shaolin Kung Fu is an art. It takes time to become an expert at an art. Also, being an artist takes individuality. You must push yourself to be the best that you can be at your art. As you give to your art, the art gives back. It will help you to better yourself.

- Train.
- Learn.
- Explore.
- Grow.
- Transform yourself.
- Shape your future.
- Reinvent yourself every day.
- Be a Shaolin Warrior.
- Be a Shaolin Athlete.

Contacting Sifu Romain

If you are planning on visiting the New York Metropolitan area, then you are invited to attend one of Sifu Romain's Shaolin Athlete/Kung Fu Conditioning courses at his academy. Be sure to contact him in advance for the opportunity to join one of his classes or to take a private lesson with him. Edgewater Kung Fu offers excellent instruction from qualified instructors in a safe, positive environment.

Edgewater Kung Fu
725 River Road
Edgewater, NJ 07020 • (201) 840-1133

You can also see what is offered at Edgewater Kung Fu by viewing the web site at www.edgewaterkungfu.com.

If you wish to inquire about Sifu Romain conducting a Shaolin Athlete/Kung Fu Conditioning Workshop at your martial art school, fitness studio, or with your sports team, then you can contact him at sifuromain@gmail.com. Continue to check www.sifuromain.com for exciting new updates. Also, check rkfsport.com for official gear and products.

APPENDICES

Appendix One

Acupuncture and the Shaolin Athlete
Written by Une-Hi Song

Traditional oriental medicine is an ancient form of healing that has been utilized for over 3,000 years. It is a holistic approach to healthcare and includes acupuncture as the primary treatment modality. Other adjunctive forms of therapy may include *tui na* (Chinese massage therapy), moxibustion (herbal heat therapy), herbs, exercise, meditation, and nutrition. Through this comprehensive medical system, a well-trained and experienced practitioner of oriental medicine treats each individual by looking at the whole person to restore and/or maintain his/her unique energetic balance.

Scientists have confirmed the close relationship between acupuncture and the involvement of the cytoskeleton, the central nervous system, lymphatic system, and the endocrine system. Hair thin needles are inserted into the body at specific points, sometimes referred to as "trigger points" or "motor points" along known pathways called meridians or channels. These needles elicit a vibratory reaction stimulating the flow of "Qi," – one's life force or vitality. Once a specific area is stimulated with the hair thin needles, they elicit a therapeutic response in the body by stimulating the flow of naturally occurring chemicals and fluids, for example, endorphins, serotonin, blood, sweat, and saliva. This essentially allows for the communication of each complex system to occur in order to achieve a healthy balance.

Complementary therapists such as acupuncturists, chiropractors, and even massage therapists are able to influence the body's natural systemic defense and repair mechanisms by manipulating and balancing these vibratory circuits.

Acupuncture is safe and virtually painless. It involves the use of hair thin needles that are inserted into specific points on the body to elicit "Qi," which usually feels like a dull ache or slight soreness. Most acupuncture patients report a feeling of relaxation or even euphoria. This may be explained by the fact that scientists have proven that the use of acupuncture triggers the release of endorphins and raises serotonin levels, which are our natural mood boosters. Endorphins have a pain relieving effect much like morphine, otherwise known as the "happy chemicals" found naturally in the human body.

Shaolin Gong Fu and Traditional Oriental Medicine have many parallels. First, they both originated in China over three thousand years ago. Second, they both center around balancing the body physically, spiritually, mentally, and emotionally as a whole unit. Third, they both center around the use of major "trigger points" on the body—the only difference being that one utilizes the points to heal and the other strikes the point to cause pain, debilitation, or even death.

Historically, Chinese military leaders were also mastermind martial arts warriors as well as healers. Oral and written history document famous stories from the battlefield about these leaders and their abilities to heal wounded soldiers and get them back into battle as quickly as possible. This was done through the use of various herbal teas, plasters, and poultices which blocked pain, stopped bleeding, and promoted tissue regeneration. Many of these ancient formulas have been passed on over the centuries and are still used today.

With all the above in mind, it is only natural that today's martial arts enthusiasts and even the "weekend warrior" would find great interest in incorporating acupuncture and herbs as part of their daily, weekly, monthly, or yearly regimen to stay healthy, happy, and injury free without narcotics or even surgery unless absolutely necessary.

Among the most extreme martial artist to the professional athlete and even to the "weekend warrior" injury is inevitable. Whether it is an acute injury (bruise, muscle tear, strain, sprain, or contusion) or chronic (tendonitis, arthritis), acupuncture and herbs are a great natural solution to recovering and/or even fully heal from minor to major injuries. The ultimate goal, just like in militant times, is to "get back to the battlefield" as quickly as possible. For us in modern times, that would be to get back to the sports we love, to work, family, and friends. We should enjoy life for all it has to offer pain free. It is important that you find a fully credentialed acupuncturist in your area. You may do so by going online to a very popular website www.acufinder.com. It is a national directory that lists only fully licensed acupuncturists by city and state and provides a complete profile containing his/her educational background, qualifications, memberships, and specialties. Most likely there will be a few to choose from, so shop around to see which one is the best fit for you.

Appendix Two

Shaolin Kung Fu and the Shaolin Athlete

Shaolin Kung Fu sounds like magic to many people, for they have learned that it is not only an effective martial art and an excellent system for health and vitality, it is also a way to spiritual joy. Those who have the privilege to meet genuine Shaolin masters or to have a more than superficial knowledge of Shaolin tradition will appreciate that this is not an exaggerated claim.[72] —Wong Kiew Kit, author of *The Art of Shaolin Kung Fu*

What is Shaolin Kung Fu? Shaolin Kung Fu was developed at the Shaolin monastery, the imperial temple located in the Sung-Shan mountain range in the Hunan Province of China. Many recognize it as being the oldest form of the Asian martial arts. In the sixth century, a Buddhist monk named Bodhidharma came from India to the Shaolin temple in China.[73] After noticing the weak physical condition of the monks, Bodhidharma introduced conditioning exercises as a means of strengthening their physical condition. This led the monks to learn self-defense techniques at the temple. These conditioning and self-defense techniques have been handed down from generation to generation over the centuries. Today, you might be familiar with some of Kung Fu's modern practitioners like Bruce Lee, Jet Li, or Jackie Chan.

Most people don't recognize what *Kung Fu* means. *Kung* means "to accomplish," and *Fu* means "effort." Together they express the idea of accomplishing a task by applying great effort. The phrase can be used to describe any aspect of life. David Chow and Richard Spangler in their excellent book, entitled, *Kung Fu: History, Philosophy, and Technique*, write, "In Western terms it can be said that Muhammad Ali achieved Kung Fu in boxing; Michelangelo attained Kung Fu in art; Ernest Hemingway reached Kung Fu in literature."[74] To achieve any great task in life requires "Kung Fu," meaning it will be accomplished with effort. So as we approach this journey as a Shaolin Athlete, we should work at it with all our heart, for that is the very meaning of Kung Fu—to accomplish with effort.

A simple definition of *Kung Fu* is "hard work." Make no mistake, Kung Fu Conditioning is hard work.

The actual word for martial arts in the Chinese is *Wu Shu*. *Wu* means "military" and *Shu* means "technique." The Chinese character for this term gives us some insight into what Wu Shu is about. David Chow and Richard Spangler write:

> The character that represents Wu Shu is composed of two parts. The first indicates the act of stopping, and the second, is a pictograph of a spear. Together they symbolize the idea of using military power to subdue violent disorder and promote peace by doing away with shields and spears. This was based on the ancient advice that "Weapons are like fire—if not extinguished they are bound to burn the user." This became a credo of the later martial artist who would not resort to using his fighting prowess whenever he wished merely to inflict harm. His art was to be used to serve and protect while avoiding conflict if at all possible.[75]

Wu Shu is a modern continuation of an ancient Chinese martial tradition. Kung Fu is also a continuation of that ancient tradition.

In *The Shaolin Athlete*, we want to share with you material that has been handed down through the centuries that will make you a better athlete and a better person. These Kung Fu Conditioning exercises have been tried and tested by ancient warriors in China and by modern-day warriors on the athletic field.

In addition, Kung Fu Conditioning draws from many different styles of Chinese martial arts. Each style contains its own forms and martial applications. Each style can be studied for years and years without exhausting the material to be learned and studied. Kung Fu Conditioning need not get stale and boring.

Internal Chinese martial arts cultivate chi. Chi is internal energy. Internal martial arts keep you young and vibrant. Chinese Chi Gong exercises have been proven to reduce stress.

The Internal Styles include:

Bagua is a circular style that focuses on waist flexibility and core strength.

Tai Chi Chuan literally means, "The Grand Ultimate Fist." Tai Chi helps with balance, breath control, flexibility, health, stress reduction, and longevity.

Hsing Xi is a linear form that develops powerful muscles, quickness, and speed.

External Chinese martial arts strengthen the muscles and get the warrior ready for combat.

The External Styles include:

Northern Long Fist Shaolin Kung Fu, which focuses on speed, power, flexibility, and agility.

Shuai-Chiao (Chinese Wresting), which conditions the whole body from head from toe.

There is a vast world of material waiting to be explored. *The Shaolin Athlete* will introduce you to this world.

Appendix Three

How Can Kung Fu Conditioning Make Me a Better Athlete?

Every athlete has to stay in top condition. Conditioning can come from running, weight training, cross-training, exercising, or playing sports. But what does Kung Fu Conditioning have to offer that other conditioning programs don't offer? Consider the benefits of Kung Fu conditioning:

1. Kung Fu Conditioning will sharpen your reflexes and response speed. Kung Fu looks for an instantaneous response from the athlete. The first two maxims in *The Eight Skills of Kung Fu* state:

Swing your fist as fast as the meteor flies.

Move your eyes as quick as lightning.

Response time in the martial arts is seen as a matter of life and death. It is taken very seriously. We train in the school as if we were in a real life or death situation. This helps develop sharp reflexes. Sharper reflexes translates into improved performance in your sport.

2. Kung Fu Conditioning will improve your focus, concentration, and clarity. When you train, you have to be in the present. This means that your mind must be absent of thought. You have to be in the moment—free of conscious thought—responding in a sub-conscious way. Master Phil Sant, Sifu Romain's instructor, calls this "*satori* of motion." *Satori* is the highest level of meditation. "Satori of motion" is the highest level of response to an outside stimulus. It is when the athlete responds and adapts without thought. Some might call this "being in the zone." Some might call this "taking over the game." Whatever you label it, Kung Fu Conditioning can help you attain this state of mental and physical conditioning. Kung Fu Conditioning helps you to play your sport at the highest level possible. It helps you play "in the zone."

3. Kung Fu Conditioning will give you functional muscles. A key to being successful in sports is having functional muscles. Functional muscles are muscles that respond appropriately to any challenge that you face. Functional muscles respond instantaneously to outside stimuli. Some training regiments give you strong muscles, but the muscles aren't functional. They are stiff and inflexible muscles. Kung Fu Conditioning strengthens the muscles, while also concentrating on the flexibility and usefulness of the muscle. This is one of the reasons why Kung Fu Conditioning is good for everyone. We all want and need functional muscles.

4. Kung Fu Conditioning includes a wide variety of techniques from many different styles of Kung Fu. Therefore, the workouts are varied and diverse. For this reason, there is less burnout and attrition than in some other conditioning programs. In Kung Fu Conditioning, there is always something new to learn. There is always a different technique to explore. Thus, Kung Fu Conditioning sharpens the mind as well as the body. The bottom line—Kung Fu Conditioning is fun. And isn't it great when work can be fun?

5. When done correctly, Kung Fu training exercises will not only strengthen the external muscles, but will also strengthen the internal organs. Kung Fu Conditioning will strengthen the body's endocrine system, the circulatory system, the skeletal system, the respiratory system and the nervous system. It will also strengthen the immune system and help with the digestion of food. Kung Fu Conditioning encompasses the athlete's whole body, inside and out.

Appendix Four

Biographies, Testimonials, and Interviews

Michael Santory

Michael Santory is a law enforcement officer who has been training with Sifu Romain since March of 2000. He currently is a 2nd degree Black Sash in Kung Fu. Mr. Santory has also studied Tai Chi.

Mr. Santory was born and raised in Brooklyn, N.Y. He grew up in the inner city where life was tough. His parents divorced when he about five months old. He lived with his mother until he was kidnapped by his father when he was five years old and taken to live with his grandmother in

Puerto Rico. He was later taken back to New York to live with his mother. Life continued to be tough for Mr. Santory. He didn't have any money to participate in team sports. Playing hand ball and stick ball on the streets of Brooklyn was his outlet. The streets were hard on his family. He eventually lost three brothers to the AIDS virus.

When asked about his greatest life achievements, Mr. Santory gave this list: graduating from college, meeting his wife on a blind date and marrying her (they've been married for nineteen years), having twin boys after five years of trying, and purchasing a house.

In March of 2000, Mr. Santory's life changed dramatically. On the same day in March he started attending the Hudson Valley Church of Christ, and he went to Nyack, New York to check out Romain's Kung Fu Academy. Mr. Santory says that training with Sifu Romain has helped him to get in the best physical condition of his life. Mr. Santory says, "I go into a training session with Sifu believing that I am in good shape, but he pushes me harder than I've ever been pushed. The techniques that he uses demand that I give my all, physically and mentally. I walk away from our training sessions challenged to do my best in every area of my life. I'm in better shape now than ever before. Sifu pushes me to the next level. He also has taught me how to be confident and how to believe in myself."

Sifu Romain has been teaching Mr. Santory to be a Kung Fu Conditioning instructor. Mr. Santory has taught Kung Fu conditioning to the baseball team at Saint Thomas Aquinas College in Sparkill, New York; to the Clarkstown South High School wrestling team in W. Nyack, New York; and to individual athletes in one-on-one training sessions. Mr. Santory says that he has noticed that, "Kung Fu Conditioning helps people's discipline. It fine tunes athletes and gives them confidence. It helps them to visualize what they can do on the field. I get the athletes to visualize that they are at the Olympics or playing in a championship game. If they can visualize doing their best off the field, then when they are on the field, they are more likely to be successful. I enjoy training other athletes. Kung Fu conditioning has helped every athlete that I have trained to be in better shape to play his or her sport."

Shane Engel, former wrestling coach at Clarkstown South High School—West Nyack, New York

Mr. Engel was born in Washington, part of the rolling farmlands of western New Jersey. He grew up fishing, hunting, and enjoying the outdoors. Washington, New Jersey is a wrestling town. Mr. Engel started wrestling when he was six years old. In fifth grade he won the state championship. He wrestled throughout high school with five other kids, and the six of them were know as "The Six Pack." ("Pack" is wrestling term for pinning the opponent). During their senior year together, these six friends won the New Jersey State Championship for their high school. For two years in a row during his high school years, Mr. Engel was ranked first in his weight class for the state of New Jersey.

After high school, Mr. Engle went on to become a scholarship athlete for the wrestling team at Rutgers University. He took fourth in the EIWA tournament his senior year in the 157 lb. weight class. Mr. Engle states that his greatest athletic achievement came during his senior year of high school when he pinned Maurice Worthy. Mr. Worthy was a the three-time New Jersey state champ who went to wrestle for the University of Oklahoma. This enabled Mr. Engel to meet Roland Gardner, the 2000 Olympic Gold medalist in wrestling. Mr. Gardner presented an award to Mr. Engel at the tournament.

When asked about his greatest life achievement, Mr. Engel quickly answered, "The greatest moment of my life came when I surrendered my life to Jesus and became a disciple." Along with being a wrestling coach, Mr. Engel is also a full-time youth minister.

Mr. Engel is the former wrestling coach for the Clarkstown South High School Vikings. Mr. Engel invited Sifu Romain to train his wrestlers in the art of Chinese wrestling (Shuai-Chiao). Sifu Romain took the wrestlers through the basic workout and drills that he shares with many of his STORM team classes on Friday night at his academies.

I (Dr. Kinnard) asked Mr. Engel, "How did you feel like the training with Sifu Romain went?" He replied, "It was great. It was very challenging to the wrestlers. It was different for them, and that's a good thing. I feel like they grew from the opportunity of training with Sifu Romain."

I asked, "What do you think your athletes were able to learn from the Kung Fu Conditioning exercises?" Mr. Engel responded, "The number one thing is mental toughness. You have to focus intensely on every single exercise that Sifu gave. If you didn't focus, then you lost your balance. The tougher it got, the more you had to focus. Working on focus intensifies your ability to focus. This was great for my wrestlers. I've been trying to get them mentally tough. When Sifu Romain was with us, it was a practice filled with mental toughness. They had to learn how to deal with pain. Learning mental toughness helps with life."

I also asked, "What else did you enjoy about Kung Fu Conditioning?" Mr. Engel responded, "Working with Sifu. He taught us a different way of training our muscles. He incorporated many different aspects of athletic conditioning like balance, speed, strength, and focus. This is unique. You rarely find conditioning exercises that work on so many different athletic attributes."

Mr. Engel added, "The emphasis that Sifu Romain placed on the phrase 'do your personal best' was very enlightening. I was glad my wrestlers heard him teach on this topic. Doing your personal best teaches you to challenge yourself regardless of what anyone around you is doing. This is the best way to train."

Appendix Five

The Eight Skills of Kung Fu

Swing your fist as fast as the meteor flies.

Move your eyes as quick as lightning.

Twist your waist as a snake.

Set your feet firm on the ground as if fastened by strong glue.

Be full of energy.

Be calm and patient.

Use your strength naturally.

Achieve your Kung Fu successfully.[76]

Helpful Mandarin Chinese Words and Phrases

A few, helpful Mandarin Chinese words and phrases. Mandarin Chinese is the language spoken at the Shaolin Temple in the Hunan Province of China.

Counting 1 to 10:
1=*Yi* (pronounced *ee*)
2=*Er* (pronounced *ehr*)
3=*San*
4=*Si* (pronounced suh)
5=*Wu*
6=*Liu* (pronounced lyoo)
7=*Qi* (pronounced chee)
8=*Ba*
9=*Jiu* (pronounced jyoo)
10=*Shi* (pronounced sher)

"Ready!"=*Yu bei!* (pronounced *yoo bay*)
"Go!"=*Zou!* (pronounced *tzo*)
Horse Stance=*Ma Bu* (pronounced *mah boo*)
Forward Stance=*Gong Bu* (pronounced *Gong boo*)
Empty Stance=*Xu Bu* (pronounced *shoo boo*)
Drop Stance=*Pu Bu* (pronounced *poo boo*)

Kung Fu Styles:

Northern Long Fist Shaolin Chuan
Bagua
Shuai-Chiao
Hsing Xi
Wing Chung
Tai Chi Chuan—literally means, "The Supreme Ultimate Fist"

ENDNOTES

1 Miyamoto Musashi, *A Book of Five Rings: A Guide to Strategy*. Translated by Victor Harris. Woodstock, New York: The Overlook Press, 1974, p. 13.

2 Forrest E. Morgan, *Living the Martial Way*. Fort Lee, New Jersey: Barricade Books, 1992, p. 24.

3 Nicklaus Suino, *Arts of Strength, Arts of Serenity: Martial Arts Training for Mental, Physical, and Spiritual Health*. New York: Weatherhill, 1996, p. 7.

4 Bruce Lee, *Tao of Jeet Kune Do*. Valencia, California. Black Belt Communications, LLC, 1975, p. 7.

5 See www.teamgiants.com/prevnews/prenews2003-8.htm.

6 ESPN, "Crouching Giant, Hidden Ninja." ESPN Internet Ventures.

7 "A Whole New Look for Giants' Toomer," by Bill Pennington, *The New York Times*, August 9, 1998.

8 "Giants' Toomer Excels With a Body of Work," by David Picker, *The New York Times*, October 18, 2007.

9 Amani Toomer, a message to the authors on Jan. 29, 2012.

10 Jeremy Booth, "Amani Toomer's Secret Weapon," from *Inside Kung Fu Magazine*. http://sifuromain.com/2003/12/01/amani-secret-weapon/.

11 Sun Tzu, *The Art of War*, http://www.military-quotes.com/Sun-Tzu.htm.

12 Sang H. Kim, *Ultimate Flexibility*. Wethersfield, Connecticut: Turtle Press, 2004, p. 20.

13 Bruce Lee, *Jeet Kune Do: Bruce Lee's Commentaries on the Martial Way*. Boston: Charles E. Tuttle Co., Inc., 1997, p. 260.

14 Bruce Lee, *Tao of Jeet Kune Do*, p. 43.

15 Morihei Ueshiba, *The Art of Peace: Teachings of the Founder of Aikido*. Complied and translated by John Stevens. Boston: Shambhala, 1992, pp. 28-29.

16 Fu Zhongwen defines the *dantian* as "a point of focus within the lower abdomen located just below the navel; associated with the physical center of gravity." The *danitan* is also considered the place where chi energy is stored. See Fu, Zhongwen, *Mastering Yang Style Taijiquan*, translated by Louis Swaim (Berkeley, California: North Atlantic Books, 1999), p. 221.

17 Lawler, Jennifer. *The Martial Arts Encyclopedia*. Indianapolis, Indiana: Masters Press, 1996, p. 85.

18 Ibid, p. 85 and p. 35.

19 A Sifu is an instructor that has reached at least a level of 5th degree black sash.

20 "The Impossible Dream," from *Man of LaMancha*, music by Mitch Leigh and lyrics by Joe Darion, published by Sam Fox Publishing Co., Inc., United Artists Records Inc., 1972.

21 Although many martial arts styles designate level advancement with belts, Kung Fu uses sashes for level advancement. The use of the sash in Kung Fu also has a practical application. The sash adds support to the stomach and intestines during training. In Kung Fu the power of the punch is derived from turning the waist. The sash provides protection to the inner organs during these violent twists. Since this curriculum is based on Kung Fu techniques, the authors often use the term "black sash" instead of "black belt." For more information on the use of the sash in Kung Fu

training see Yang Jwing-Ming and Jeffery A. Bolt's *Shaolin Long Fist Kung Fu*, Burbank, CA.: Unique Publications, 1982, pp. 21-22.

22 Shinichi Suzuki, *Nurtured by Love: The Classic Approach to Talent Education*. Translated by Waltraud Suzuki. Second Edition. Miami: Warner Brothers Publications Inc., 1983, p. 15.

23 The STORM Team is made up of students who have decided they want to train to become instructors. CIT stands for Chief Instructor Training. This training not only prepares you to be an instructor but to be a martial arts professional and lead a martial arts academy.

24 Suzuki, p. 66.

25 Ibid., p. 83.

26 Bruce Lee, *Tao of Jeet Kune Do*. Balencia, CA: Black Belt Communications LLC, 1975, p. 27.

27 *The Journal News*. LoHud.com. Owned by Gannet Inc.

28 See Stephen R. Covey, *The 8th Habit: From Effectiveness to Greatness*. New York: Free Press, 2004. This is an excellent book. We highly recommend it and Covey's other book, *The Seven Habits of Highly Effective People*. We often refer to these books in our Kung Fu Conditioning program.

29 Dr. Laurence J. Peter, http://www.quotationspage.com/quotes/Laurence J. Peter.

30 The Ford Foundation, http://www.ideamarketers.com/?Only 3 percent Of People Achieve Their Goals&articleid=417771.

31 James E. Loehr, *Toughness Training For Life*. New York: Plume, 1993, p. 193.

32 Covey, *The 8th Habit*, p. 70.

33 Loehr, p. 194.

34 Covey, *The 8th Habit*, p. 70.

35 Loehr, p. 7.

36 Covey, *The 8th Habit*, p. 75.

37 Suzuki, Shunryu. *Zen Mind, Beginner's Mind*. New York: Weatherhill, 1970, p. 21.

38 Michael L. Raposa, *Meditation and the Martial Arts*. Charlottesville, Virginia: University of Virginia Press, 2003, p. 78.

39 Ueshiba, p. 23.

40 Bruce Lee, *Jeet Kune Do: Bruce Lee's Commentaries on the Martial Way*. Boston: Charles E. Tuttle Co., Inc., 1997, p. 363.

41 Michael Jordan, http://www.brainyquote.com/quotes/quotes/m/michaeljor127660.html.

42 Mike Ditka, http://quotesou.w06.winhost.com/famous_quotes/quote.aspx?id=48909

43 Loehr, p. 7.

44 Dee Hock, found in Covey, *The 8th Habit*, p. 58.

45 Bruce Lee with John Little as editor. *Bruce Lee: Artist of Life*. Boston: Tuttle Publishing, 1999, p. 259.

46 Musashi, pp. 51-52.

47 Suino, p. 38

48 As found in Stephen Covey's *The Seven Habits of Highly Effective People*.

49 Joe Hyams, *Zen in the Martial Arts*. New York: Penguin Putnam, Inc., 1979, p. 9.

50 Musashi, p. 8.

51 Musashi, p. 36.

52 This is a paraphrase of Proverbs 23:7.

53 Tsung Hwa Jou. *The Dao of Taijiquan: Way to Rejuvenation*. Scottsdale, Arizona: Tai Chi Foundation, 2001, p. 15.

54 Bruce Lee, *Jeet Kune Do*, p. 328.

55 Musashi, p. 8.

56 Dennis Waitley, http://www.inspirationalquotes4u.com/waitleyquotes/index.html.

57 Michael L. Raposa. *Meditation and the Martial Arts*. Charlottesville, Virginia: University of Virginia Press, 2003, p. 75.

58 Ueshiba, p. 45.

59 Raposa, p. 40.

60 Herman Kauz. *A Path to Liberation: A Spiritual and Philosophical Approach to the Martial Arts*. Woodstock, New York: Overlook Press, 1992, p. 26.

61 Raposa , p. 9.

62 Paul could have been speaking literally or figuratively here. Scholars are divided on this issue.

63 Ueshiba, p. 41.

64 Source Unknown.

65 John Schaar, http://www.memorable-quotes.com/john+schaar,a4643.html.

66 Covey, *The 8th Habit*, p. 48.

67 Covey, *The 8th Habit*, p. 58.

68 Kent M. Keith as found in Stephen R. Covey, *The 8th Habit*, p. 80.

69 Loehr, p. 59.

70 Morgan, p.

71 Nicklaus Suino. Arts of Strength, *Arts of Serenity: Martial Arts Training for Mental, Physical, and Spiritual Health*. New York: Weatherhill, 1996, p. 13.

72 Wong Kiew Kit, *The Art of Shaolin Kung Fu*. Boston: Tuttle Publishing, 2002, p. xvi.

73 Bodhidharma is also know as Da Bo. Four techniques that are attributed to Bodhidharma are the *WuXing Quan* (the five animal forms), the *Louhan Shi Ba Shou* (the 18 Louhan Palms), the *Yi Jin Jing* (muscle and tendon changing), and *Xi Sui Jing* (bone-marrow washing).

74 David Chow and Richard Spangler. *Kung Fu: History, Philosophy and Technique*. Burbank, California: Unique Publications, 1982, p. xi.

75 Ibid, p. xii.

76 Source unknown.

BIBLIOGRAPHY

Belonoha, Wayne. *The Wing Chun Compendium*. Berkeley, California: Blue Snake Books, 2004, 2006.

Benton, Sue and Drew Denbaum. *Chi Fitness: A Workout for Body, Mind, and Spirit*. New York: Quill, A HarperResource Book, 2001.

Bracy, John and Xing-Han Liu. *Ba Gua: Hidden Knowledge in the Taoist Internal Martial Art*. Berkeley, California: North Atlantic Books, 1998.

Cao, Yimin. "How Taiji Enhances the Quality of Life." T'ai Chi. Vol. 29, No. 4 (August 2005): 14–24.

Carnegie, Dale. *How to Win Friends and Influence People*. New York: Simon and Schuster, 1937.

Chen, Mei-June and Martha Burr. *Shaolin Ulysses: Kungfu Monks in America*. (Film). Lotus Film Group, 2003.

Chen, William C. C. *Body Mechanics of T'ai Chi*. New York: William C. C. Chen Publisher, 1973.

Chen, Yearning K. *Tai Chi Churan—Its Effects and Practical Applications*. Los Angeles: Ohara Publications, [n.d.].

Cheng Man-ch'ing. *Master Cheng's Thirteen Chapters on T'ai Chi Ch'uan*. Translated by Douglas Wile. Brooklyn, New York: Sweet Ch'i Press, 1982.

_____. *T'ai Chi Ch'uan: A Simplified Method of Calisthenics and Self Defense*. Berkeley , California: North Atlantic Books, 1981.

Cheng Man-ch'ing and Robert W. Smith. *T'ai Chi: The "Supreme Ultimate" Exercise for Health, Sport, and Self-Defense*. Boston: Tuttle Publishing, 1966.

Cheung, William. *Kung Fu Dragon Pole*. Burbank, California: Ohara Publications, 1986.

_____, *Advanced Wing Chun*. Burbank, California: Ohara Publications, 1988.

Chow, David and Richard Spangler. *Kung Fu: History, Philosophy and Technique*. Burbank, California: Unique Publications, 1982.

Chu, C.K. *Tai Chi Chuan: Principles & Practice*. New York: Sunflower Press, 2006.

Chuang Tzu. *Chuang Tzu: Basic Writings*. Translated by Burton Watson. New York: Columbia University Press, 1996.

_____. *The Complete Works of Chuang Tzu*. New York: Columbia University Press, 1968.

Chuckrow, Robert. *The Tai Chi Book*. Boston: YMAA Publication Center, 1998.

Cleary, Thomas, transl. *Code of the Samurai: A Modern Translation of the Bushido Shoshinshu of Taira Shigesuke*. Rutland, Vermont: Tuttle Publishing, 1999.

Collins, Jim and Jerry I. Porras. *Built to Last: Successful Habits of Visionary Companies*. New York: CollinsBusiness Essentials, 1994.

Collins, Jim. *Good to Great: Why Some Companies Make the Leap...and Others Don't*. New York: Harper Business, 2001.

Covey, Stephen R. *The 7 Habits of Highly Effective People: Restoring the Character Ethic*. New York: Free Press, 1989.

_____. *The 8th Habit: From Effectiveness to Greatness*. New York: Free Press, 2004.

Craig, Darrell Max. *Japan's Ultimate Martial Art*. Boston: Charles E. Tuttle Co., 1995.

Deshimaru, Taisen. *The Zen Way To The Martial Arts*. Translated by Nancy Amphoux. New York: E. P. Dutton Inc., 1979.

Diffenderffer, Bill. *The Samurai Leader*. Naperville, Illinois: Sourcebooks, Inc., 2005.

Draeger, Donn F. and Robert W. Smith. *Comprehensive Asian Fighting Arts*. Tokyo: Kodansha International Ltd., 1986.

Dreyer, Danny with Katherine Dreyer. *Chi Running*. New York: Simon & Schuster, 2004.

Frantzis, B. K. *Opening the Energy Gates of Your Body*. Berkeley, California: North Atlantic Books, 1993.

_____. *The Power of Internal Martial Arts*. Berkeley, California: North Atlantic Books, 1998.

Fu, Zhongwen. *Mastering Yang Style Taijiquan*. Translated by Louis Swaim. Berkeley, California: North Atlantic Books, 1999.

Galante, Lawrence. *Tai Chi—The Supreme Ultimate*. York Beach, Maine: Samuel Weiser, 1981.

Glover, Bob, Jack Shepherd, and Shelly-Lynn Florence Glover. *The Runner's Handbook*. New York: Penguin Books, 1996.

Hallander, Jane. *The Complete Guide to Kung Fu Fighting Styles*. [n.p.]: Unique Publications, 1985.

Henderson, Joe. *Run Right Now*. New York: Barnes & Noble Books, 2004.

Henning, Stanley E. "Insights From the Home of Xingyiquan." *Journal of Asian Martial Arts* Vol. 14, No. 3 (2005).

Higdon, Hal. *Marathon: The Ultimate Training Guide*. [n.p.]: Rodale, 1999.

Hsu, Adam. *A Sword Polisher's Record: The Way of Kung-Fu*. Boston: Tuttle Publishing, 1997.

Jones, Charlotte. "Studies on the Health Benefits of Tai Chi." T'ai Chi. Vol. 30, No. 4 (August 2006): 14–20.

Jou, Tsung Hwa. *The Dao of Taijiquan: Way to Rejuvenation*. Scottsdale, Arizona: Tai Chi Foundation, 2001.

_____. *The Tao of I Ching: Way to Divination*. Scottsdale, Arizona: Tai Chi Foundation, 1983.

_____. *The Tao of Meditation: Way to Enlightenment*. Scottsdale, Arizona: Tai Chi Foundation, 1983.

Kaufman, Stephen F. *The Martial Artist's Book of Five Rings: The Definitive Interpretation of Miyamoto Musashi's Classic Book of Strategy*. Boston: Tuttle Publishing, 1994.

Kauz, Herman. *A Path to Liberation: A Spiritual and Philosophical Approach to the Martial Arts*. Woodstock, New York: Overlook Press, 1992.

Khor, Gary. *Reflections on Qi: Turning Your Life to the World's Hidden Energy*. Sydney: New Holland Publishers, 2004.

Kim, Sang H. *Ultimate Flexibility*. Wethersfield, Connecticut: Turtle Press, 2004.

Kinnard, G. Steve. *The Beginning of Wisdom*. New York: The New York City Church of Christ, 1988.

_____. *The Call of the Wise: An Introduction and Topical Index to the Book of Proverbs*. Woburn, Massachusetts: Discipleship Publications International, 1997.

_____. *The Crowning of the King: A Practical Exposition of the Gospel of Matthew*. Newton, Massachusetts: Illuminations Publishers International, 2004.

_____. *The Final Act: A Biblical Look at End-Time Prophecy*. Woburn, Massachusetts: Discipleship Publications International, 2000.

_____. *Getting the Most From the Bible*. Woburn, Massachusetts: Discipleship Publications International, 2000.

_____. *The Gospel of Mark: An Introduction to Discipleship*. Woburn, Massachusetts: Discipleship Publications International, 1995.

_____. *Holy Land Tour: The Gihon Spring*. (Video). New City, New York: G. Steve Kinnard, 2000.

_____. *Jerusalem: City of Promise.* (Video). New City, New York: G. Steve Kinnard, 1999.

_____. *New Wineskins: Formation of a Ministry of Multimedia Education Integrating the Bible, Geography and Archaeology.* New City: New York: G. Steve Kinnard, 1999.

_____. *Prophets: The Voices of Yahweh.* Billerica, Massachusetts: Discipleship Publications International, 2001.

Kong, Buck-sam. *The Tiger/Crane Form of Hung Gar Kung Fu.* Santa Clarita: Ohara Publication, 1983.

Kong, Buck-sam, and Eugene H. Ho. *Hung Gar Kung Fu.* Burbank, California: Ohara Publications, 1972.

Laing, Shou-Yu and Yang Jwing-Ming. *Xingyiquan: Theory, Applications, Fighting Tactics, and Spirit.* Boston: YMAA Publication Center, 2002.

Laing, T. T. *T'ai Chi Ch'uan: For Health and Self-Defense.* New York: Vintage Books, 1977.

Lao, Tzu. *Tao Te Ching.* New York: Penguin Books, 1963.

Lawler, Jennifer. *The Martial Arts Encyclopedia.* Indianapolis, Indiana: Masters Press, 1996.

Lee, Bruce. *Chinese Gong Fu, the Philosophical Art of Self-Defense.* Oakland, California: Oriental Book Sales, 1963.

_____. *Tao of Jeet Kune Do.* Valencia, California.: Black Belt Communications, LLC, 1975.

Lee, Bruce, with John Little as editor. *Bruce Lee: Artist of Life.* Boston: Tuttle Publishing, 1999.

_____. *Jeet Kune Do: Bruce Lee's Commentaries on the Martial Way.* Boston: Charles E. Tuttle Co., Inc., 1997.

_____. *Letters of the Dragon: Correspondence 1957–1973.* Boston: Tuttle Publishing, 1998.

_____. *The Tao of Gong Fu.* Boston: Tuttle Publishing, 1997.

Lee, Bruce, and M. Uyehara. *Bruce Lee's Fighting Methods: Volume One, Self-Defense Techniques.* Burbank, California.: Ohara Publications, 1976.

_____. *Bruce Lee's Fighting Methods: Volume Two, Basic Training.* Burbank, California: Ohara Publications, 1976.

_____. *Bruce Lee's Fighting Methods: Volume Three, Skill in Techniques.* Burbank, California: Ohara Publications, 1976.

_____. *Bruce Lee's Fighting Methods: Volume Four, Advanced Techniques.* Burbank, California: Ohara Publications, 1976.

Lee, James Y. *Wing Chun Kung Fu.* Burbank, California: Ohara Publications, 1975.

Leung Ting. *Seven Star Praying Mantis Kung Fu.* Hong Kong: International Wing Tsun Leung Ting Martial Arts Association, 1980.

_____. *Skills of the Vagabonds.* Hong Kong: Leung's Publications, 1983.

_____. *Skills of the Vagabonds II: Behind the Incredibles.* Hong Kong: Leung's Publications, 1991.

Lewis, Peter. *Myths and Legends of the Martial Arts.* London: Prion Books Limited, 1998.

Little, John R. *Bruce Lee: A Warrior's Journey.* Chicago: Contemporary Books, 2001.

Loehr, James E. *Toughness Training For Life.* New York: Plume, 1993.

Lowry, Dave. *Moving Toward Stillness.* Boston: Tuttle Publishing, 2000.

Lu Shengli. *Combat Techniques of Taiji, Xingyi, and Bagua: Principles and Practices of Internal Martial Arts.* Translated by Zhang Yun. Berkeley, California: Blue Snake Books, 2006.

Maliszewski, Michael. *Spiritual Dimensions of the Martial Arts.* Rutland, Vermont: Charles E. Tuttle Company, 1996.

Maxwell, John C. *Be A People Person: Effective Leadership Through Effective Relationships.* Colorado Springs, Colorado:1994.

_____.*The Winning Attitude: Your Pathway to Personal Success.* Nashville, Tennessee: Thomas Nelson Publishers, 1993.

McMahon, John. *"Art of Leadership: Applying Aikido Principles to Business."* Black Belt. Vol. 43, No. 9 (September 2005): 85–90.

Merton, Thomas. *The Way of Chuang Tzu.* New York: New Directions, 1965.

Mishima, Yukio. *Hagakure Nyumon (The Way of the Samurai).* Translated by Kathryn Sparling. New York: Basic Books, 1977.

Mitose, James M. *What Is Self Defense? (Kenpo Jiu-Jitsu).* Sacramento, California: Kosho-Shorei Publishing Co., 1953.

Morgan, Forrest E. *Living the Martial Way.* Fort Lee, New Jersey: Barricade Books, 1992.

Morrissey, Linda. *Introduction to Yang Style Tai Chi Chuan—Part One.* (Video). Nyack, New York: Linda Morrissey, 2002.

_____. *Introduction to Yang Style Tai Chi Chuan—Part Two.* (Video). Nyack, New York: Linda Morrissey, 2002.

Musashi, Miyamoto. *A Book of Five Rings: A Guide to Strategy.* Translated by Victor Harris. Woodstock, New York: The Overlook Press, 1974.

Order of Shaolin Ch'an. *The Shaolin Grandmasters' Text: History, Philosophy, and Gong Fu of Shaolin Ch'an.* Revised Edition. Beaverton, Oregon: Order of Shaolin Ch'an. 2004, 2006.

Pang-Jeng Lo, Benjamin, editor. *The Essence of T'ai Chi Ch'uan: The Literary Tradition.* Berkeley, California: North Atlantic Books, 1985.

Parker, Edmund. *Ed Parker's Infinite Insights into Kenpo. Volume 1: Mental Stimulation.* Los Angeles: Delsby Publications, 1982.

_____. *Ed Parker's Infinite Insights into Kenpo. Volume 2: Physical Analyzation I.* Los Angeles: Delsby Publications, 1983.

_____. *Ed Parker's Infinite Insights into Kenpo. Volume 3: Physical Analyzation II.* Los Angeles: Delsby Publications, 1985.

_____. *Ed Parker's Infinite Insights into Kenpo. Volume 4: Mental & Physical Constituents.* Los Angeles: Delsby Publications, 1986.

_____. *Ed Parker's Infinite Insights into Kenpo. Volume 5: Mental & Physical Applications.* Los Angeles: Delsby Publications, 1987.

_____. *Law of the Fist And The Empty Hand.* Los Angeles: Delsby Publications, 1960.

_____. *Secrets of Chinese Karate.* Englewood Cliffs, New Jersey: Prentice-Hall, 1963.

Payne, Peter. *Martial Arts: The Spiritual Dimension.* New York: Crossroads, 1981.

Polly, Matthew. *American Shaolin.* New York: Gotham Books, 2007.

P'ng Chye Khim and Donn Fr. Draeger. *Shaolin Lohan Kung-Fu.* Tokyo: Tuttle, 1979.

Raposa, Michael L. *Meditation and the Martial Arts.* Charlottesville, Virginia: University of Virginia Press, 2003.

Romain, Karl. *Advanced Sparring.* (Video). Nyack, New York: Kurom Martial Arts, Inc., 2005.

_____. *Broadsword.* (Video). Nyack, New York: Kurom Martial Arts, Inc., 2005.

_____. *Bully Safe.* (Video). [n.p.]: Bully Safe LLC., 2001.

_____. *Chin Na.* (DVD). Nyack, New York: Kurom Martial Arts, Inc., 2005.

_____. *Lohan: Eighteen Hands.* (Video). Nyack, New York: Kurom Martial Arts, Inc., 2005.

_____. *Legendary Long Fist.* (Book). Nyack, New York: Kurom Martial Arts, Inc., 2005.

_____. *Shaolin Long Fist Form I.* (DVD). Nyack, New York: Kurom Martial Arts, Inc., 2005.

_____. *Shaolin Long Fist Form II.* (DVD). Nyack, New York: Kurom Martial Arts, Inc., 2005.

_____. *Shaolin Self-Defense Techniques, Part 1.* (DVD). Nyack, New York: Kurom Martial Arts, Inc., 2000.

_____. *Shaolin Self-Defense Techniques, Part 2.* (DVD). Nyack, New York: Kurom Martial Arts, Inc., 2000.

Shaolin Gong Fu Institute. www.shaolin.com

Shaw, Scott. *The Warrior Is Silent.* Rochester, Vermont: Inner Traditions, 1998.

Smith, Robert W. and Allen Pittman. *Pa-Kua: Eight-Trigram Boxing.* Boston: Tuttle Publishing, 1990.

_____. *Hsing-I: Chinese Internal Boxing.* Rutland, Vermont: Charles E. Tuttle Company, Inc., 1990.

Smith, Robert W. *Chinese Boxing: Masters and Methods.* Berkeley, California: North Atlantic Books, 1990.

_____. *Martial Musings: A Portrayal of Martial Arts in the 20th Century.* Erie, Pennsylvania: Via Media Publishing Company, 1999.

_____. *Pa-Kua: Chinese Boxing For Fitness and Self-Defense.* Tokyo: Kodansha International Ltd., 1967.

Soho, Takuan. *The Unfettered Mind.* Translated by William Scott Wilson. New York: Kodansha International Ltd., 2002.

Sprackland, Robert. *Instructor: Teaching the Martial Arts.* Belmont, California: Young Forest Company, 1998.

Sun Tzu. *The Art of War.* Translated by Ralph D. Sawyer. New York: Barnes & Nobles Books, 1994.

Suino, Nicklaus. *Arts of Strength, Arts of Serenity: Martial Arts Training for Mental, Physical, and Spiritual Health.* New York: Weatherhill, 1996.

Suzuki, Shinichi. *Nurtured by Love: The Classic Approach to Talent Education.* Translated by Waltraud Suzuki. Second Edition. Miami: Warner Brothers Publications Inc., 1983.

Suzuki, Shunryu. *Zen Mind, Beginner's Mind.* New York: Weatherhill, 1970.

T'ai Chi Ch'uan. Published by the T'ai Chi Ch'uan Association to commemorate its third anniversary in 1968.

T'ai Chi Classics. Translated and with additional commentary by Waysun Liao. Boston: Shambhala, 1990.

T'ai-Chi Touchstones: Yang Family Secret Transmissions. Compiled and translated by Douglas Wile. Revised edition. Brooklyn, New York: Sweet Ch'i Press, 1983.

Tang, Sun Lu. *Xing Yi Quan Xue: The Study of Form-Mind Boxing.* Burbank, California: Unique Publications, 2000.

Tom, Teri. *The Straight Lead.* Rutland, Vermont: Tuttle Publishing, 2005.

Ueshiba, Morihei. *The Art of Peace: Teachings of the Founder of Aikido.* Complied and translated by John Stevens. Boston: Shambhala, 1992.

_____. *Budo: Teachings of the Founder of Aikido.* Translated by John Stevens. Tokyo: Kodansha International, 1991.

Uyehara, M. *Bruce Lee: The Incomparable Fighter.* Santa Clara, California: Ohara Publications Inc., 1998.

Ultimate Martial Arts Encyclopedia: The Best of Inside Kung-Fu. Edited by John R. Little and Curtis F. Wong. Lincolnwood, Illinois: Contemporary Books, 2000.

Whitsett, David A., Forrest A. Dolgener, and Tanjala Moabon Kole. *The Non-Runner's Marathon Trainer.* New York: McGraw-Hill, 1998.

Wile, Douglas. *Lost T'ai Ch'I Classics from the Late Ch'ing Dynasty.* Albany, New York: State University of New York Press, 1996.

_____. *Introduction to Shaolin Kung Fu.* London: Paul H. Crompton, Ltd., 1994.

Wilson, William Scott. *The Lone Samurai: The Life of Miyamoto Musashi.* Tokyo: Kodansha International, 2004.

Wong, James I., editor. *A Source Book in the Chinese Martial Arts, Volume I: History, Philosophy, Systems, and Styles.* Stockton, California: Koinonia, 1978.

Wong, Kiew Kit. *The Art of Shaolin Kung Fu: The Secrets of Kung Fu for Self-Defense, Health, and Enlightenment.* Boston: Tuttle Publishing, 2002.

_____. *Introduction to Shaolin Kung Fu.* London: Paul H. Crompton, Ltd., 1994.

Wooden, John with Steve Jamison. *Wooden: A Lifetime of Observations and Reflections On and Off the Court.* Chicago: Contemporary Books, 1997.

Yamamoto, Tsunetomo. *Hagakure: The Book of the Samurai.* Translated by William Scott Nelson. Tokyo: Kodansha International, 1979.

Yang Chengfu. *The Essence and Applications of Tajiquan.* Translated by Louis Swaim. Berkeley, California: North Atlantic Books, 2005.

Yang Jwing-Ming. *Advanced Yang Style Tai Chi Chuan, Volume 1, Tai Chi Theory and Tai Chi Jing.* Boston: Yang's Martial Arts Academy, 1986.

_____. *Advanced Yang Style Tai Chi Chuan, Volume 2, Martial Applications.* Boston: Yang's Martial Arts Academy, 1986.

_____. *Muscle/Tendon Changing and Marrow/Brain Washing Chi Kung—The Secret of Youth.* Jamaica Plain, Massachusetts: Yang's Martial Arts Association, 1989.

_____. *QiGong For Health and Martial Arts: Exercises and Meditation.* Boston: Yang's Martial Arts Academy, 1988.

_____ and Jeffery A. Bolt. *Shaolin Long Fist Kung Fu.* Burbank, California: Unique Publications, Inc., 1982.

Yang, Yang, with Scott A. Grubisich, *Taijiquan: The Art of Nurturing, The Science of Power.* Champaign, Illinois: Zhenwu Publications, 2005.

Yang Zhen-Duo, *Traditional Yang Family Style Taijiquan.* Winchester, Virgina: A Taste of China, Inc., 1991.

Ying Zi, and Weng Yi. *Shaolin Kung Fu.* Kowloon: Kingsway International, 1981.

Yumoto, John M. *The Samurai Sword: A Handbook.* Boston: Tuttle Publishing, 1958.

Zhang Yun. *The Art of Chinese Swordsmanship: A Manual of Taiji Jian.* Boston: Weatherhill, 1998.

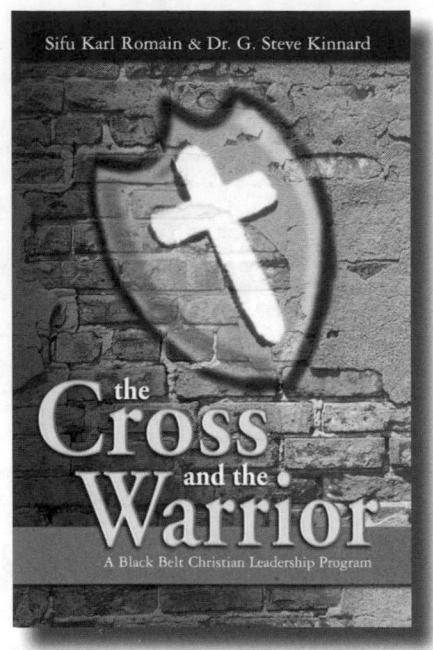

The Cross and the Warrior
by Sifu Karl Romain and Dr. G. Steve Kinnard

ISBN: 978-0-9776954-7-6
Price: $8.00, 102 page instructional book.

The Cross and the Warrior is a Black Belt Christian Leadership Training Program developed by Sifu Karl Romain and Dr. G. Steve Kinnard. The goal of this program is to teach leadership principles through martial arts training. This course has been developed for at-risk pre-teen and teenage boys and girls. But the course can be adapted to any age group. This book shows you how to teach inspirational leadership lessons while challenging students in martial arts training.

"Karl Romain has successfully connected man's faith in God with the discipline of the art of Kung Fu..."
   Howard Cross—played in the most games in New York Giants football
      history and is a student of Karl Romain.

"Sifu Romain and Dr. Kinnard are right on the money with this. It especially appeals to urban teens that are hard to engage."
   Lawton "Bud" Chiles—CEO of Chiles Florida Assets

Theatron Press
www.Theatron-Press.com
www.ipibooks.com
Also available on www.Amazon.com